HOPI DYES

mary~russell ferrell colton

foreword by marsha gallagher

Museum of Northern Arizona Press • Flagstaff

Dedicated to the
Hopi People

Table of Contents

Foreword

THIS NEW ISSUE of Mary-Russell Ferrell Colton's book on Hopi dyes comes at an opportune time. Interest in the use of natural dyes of all kinds has been growing steadily, and amateur and professional craftsmen alike are sure to welcome having this major resource readily available again. The publication also coincides with the fiftieth anniversary of the Museum of Northern Arizona and is a fitting tribute to Mrs. Colton, who, with her husband, was a cofounder of this institution.

An artist herself, Mrs. Colton guided the art interests of the Museum for many years. She planned new exhibits, acquired objects for the collections, and devoted much time and energy to various research and education projects. One of these projects was her detailed study of Hopi dyes. She spent many years discussing dyeing techniques with Hopi artisans, collecting native dyestuffs, and running laboratory experiments to determine proper "recipes." The result was a clearly written compendium of information on Hopi dyes, first published in 1965.

This new issue retains the text and format of the original, which was meant to be a permanent record of Hopi knowledge and was written as a handbook for use by future Hopi dyers. There have, however, been three additions to the 1965 edition: a new cover, a set of color plates, and a list of additional suggested readings. The photographs have been included to show the variety of naturally produced hues that have been and still are being used by Hopi craftsmen to color their textiles and especially their basketry. The suggested readings should be helpful to those who want to learn more about dyeing with natural materials.

Some home dyers may find it difficult or impractical to exactly duplicate the ingredients and procedures outlined in *Hopi Dyes*. While reasonable cautions should be employed (some mordants and plants are poisonous), a dyer's own experience will allow for experimentation and substitution. For example, as a mordant, commercial alum (potassium aluminum sulfate) could be substituted for the native type, but the quantity used would vary. In some instances household ammonia might be used in place of urine in the dying process, as in a final rinse or bath; in other cases, such as indigo dyeing, ammonia would not be an advisable substitute. As for dyestuffs, related plant species or varieties can sometimes be used interchangeably. The results may approach those of the Hopi dyes. One experiment with a commercial red corn yielded a hue similar to that produced by *koko' ma*, but a substitution of commercial sunflower seeds for the native variety was not nearly so successful. However, in vegetable dyeing no two dyebaths, even those using the same recipe, are ever exactly alike. Variation in color is part of the challenge and fascination of working with natural materials. In fact, this is one of the principal pleasures in working from a book like *Hopi Dyes*.

1978   Marsha Gallagher

                                         Registrar of Anthropology
                                         Museum of Northern Arizona

Introduction

THE WORK DESCRIBED in this paper has covered many years, mostly between 1930 and 1945, first in the field and then in the laboratory.

It is written primarily for the Hopi themselves and especially for the "young people" who, in a rapidly changing world, tend to forget the accomplishments and discoveries of their own people.

The "recipes" presented in this paper have all been tested by the writer and assembled in a workable form. The materials used and their treatment in the laboratory follow primitive procedure as closely as possible. These procedures are "time consuming" and as "time" today is extremely valuable, the Hopi dyer need have no fear that his art will ever be commercialized.

The writer is a painter and technician, a graduate of the Philadelphia School of Design for Women, now called the Moore Institute of Art and Industry. She served as Curator of Art at the Museum of Northern Arizona from 1928 to 1952. From 1952 to 1963 she was Chairman of the Arts Committee of the Board of Trustees of the Northern Arizona Society of Science and Art, Inc., which operates the Museum.

At the Museum, special emphasis was placed on the maintenance and encouragement of Indian Art. The first "Hopi Craftsman" exhibition was held in July, 1930. These annual exhibitions still continue and are held each year at the same time.

The background work in the field for the exhibitions was of special importance and has yielded information not previously recorded.

Every year many trips were made to the Hopi villages where

we lived in the homes of the people or camped nearby. When the Hopi understood what we wished to do, they taught us many things and insisted that we learn the correct procedures. Many of the processes described here have, in the past, been regarded as the property of certain clans, families or individuals and are practiced in a secret manner. Thus, with the death of an individual or passing of a clan, much knowledge was lost, and remained with the people, only as a vague rumor.

The writer gratefully wishes to acknowledge the understanding cooperation of the Hopi craftsmen, men and women, old and young. They have enabled us to record their knowledge and use of vegetable dyes, minerals, and stains permanently for them in this book.

The dye plants were identified by Mr. A. F. Whiting and published by the Museum of Northern Arizona, Bull. 15, 1939.

CHAPTER I

Prehistoric Dyes

THE PREHISTORIC PUEBLOAN PEOPLES of the Southwest were master craftsmen. Expert weavers and dyers, basket makers and potters, their arts were varied, colorful and thriving, when History first discovered them in New Mexico and Arizona.

From the earliest Spanish records to the American invasion, old documents abound in references to the arts of these peoples, whom the Conquistadors marveled to find living in cities and practicing the "civilized arts."*

As the Spaniards themselves were no mean artisans, we may judge that the arts of the Puebloans were highly developed and enjoying a period of "Renaissance." "Embroidered and painted cotton textiles" are frequently mentioned, and also the quality and abundance of the large ollas and beautiful painted bowls.

The prehistory of the "Cultural Ancestors" of these people, is slowly revealing the early pueblo dweller and his fore-runner, the "Basketmaker," as artisans of remarkable skill and invention, to whom the craftsman of today cannot compare, for in most cases he cherishes only vague memories of past skills.

In the Basketmaker period, 500 to 700 A.D., the ancestors of the Hopi, not yet possessing cotton, skilfully wove and dyed yucca and other vegetable fibers, fashioning these harsh materials into clothing, sandals, matting and baskets of great beauty.

Then came cotton, the most precious of all vegetable fibers in the New World. At first, it must have been scarce, for we see it used sparingly, combined with coarser fibers. Finally it appears alone, as the main textile fiber of the prehistoric Puebloan while

* Kent, 1957, pp. 478-483, 487.

the other vegetable fibers take their place for basketry, sandals, matting, etc.

With the coming of a white fiber like cotton, the dyer's art must have received a great impetus, for it made possible the use of an infinite number of shades not effective upon the darker fibers.

This was apparently the case, for spun cotton textiles embellished with designs in shades of rust, red, orange, yellow, brown, black, dull blues and purples have been recorded from excavated material.

These conditions apparently continued to flourish up to the advent of the Spaniard.

There was definitely no wide-spread decadence in the arts from the Basketmaker to the historic period, but rather a steady progression toward a general "Renaissance" of Puebloan arts.

With the coming of a new race, there also arrived a strange new animal, the sheep, whose advent completely changed the textile industries of the Puebloan and stimulated the nomadic Navajo to adopt the arts of their sedentary neighbors. When the Pueblo people acquired sheep from their Spanish conquerors and found that the long white fibers of wool could be spun and woven into excellent cloth and with far less exertion than required for cotton, the next step was naturally the decoration by coloring of these new fibers.

Therefore, it is reasonable to suppose that a Hopi, upon receiving new material which he wanted to dye, would first try upon this material, the dyes and mordants with which he was familiar in the dying of cotton. We may find in use today only those dyes which could be adapted to wool, by the use of mordants already known to the people and formerly used for cotton, even though such dyes may require different adjustments in treatment for the new fiber.

However, it is certain that the Hopi, lineal descendants of the prehistoric basket makers of this region, still use, with equal success upon either wool or cotton, and other plant fibers, most of the old dyes. The shades produced, however, vary considerably on the various fibers.

The introduction of aniline dyes about 1880* was a severe check upon the native dye industry, both Hopi and Navajo, though it

* Amsden, 1934, p. 88.

would seem that native dyes never came as near complete extinction among the Hopi as with the Navajo. This, however, has not been fully realized, owing to the fact that there are so few Hopi textiles on the market and that the Hopi carry on an extensive intertribal trade.

The revival of Indian arts in the 1930's, for which the Museum of Northern Arizona has been working among the Hopi, has stimulated the people to renewed interest in their ancient crafts and to a lively experimentation with dyes and mordants.

Transcribing Hopi words into English

The spelling of Hopi words with our English alphabet offers some difficulties. We have adopted in this work the following rules: the vowels have continental values such as in German, French, or Spanish; the consonants, as in English, except *q* without *u* is used for *k* sound further back in the throat than the English *k*. The Hopi language has no *b, d, g, rz,* or *sh,* and it distinguishes between long and short vowels: between short vowels, *a* and between long vowels, *a:.* A glottal stop is ' and an accent is '.

Hopi woman demonstrates plaque-making.

CHAPTER II

Textile and Basketry Objects

THE FOLLOWING ARTICLES were being manufactured in the pueblos in 1954, but no claim is made that this is a complete list.

Textiles Worn by Women

1. Wedding robe: hand spun white cotton, basket weave.
2. Wedding belt: hand spun white cotton, braided.
3. Maiden's shawl: white wool or cotton with red border, diagonal basket weave.
4. Woman's ceremonial dress: made from small wedding robe and heavily embroidered in colored wool yarns.
5. Woman's dress: diamond, diagonal weave, dark blue and black.
6. Woman's belt: red, floated patterns in black and green.
7. Woman's (sometimes men's) footless stockings or leggings: black or white; knit in several patterns by the men.

Textiles Worn by Small Children (textiles for children are always black and white)

8. Baby's blanket: wool, basket weave.
9. Boy's shoulder blanket: two sizes, black and white plaid design, basket weave.

Textiles Worn by Men

10. Ceremonial sash: wool or cotton, basket weave, brocaded in colored wools.
11. Ceremonial kilt: hand spun white cotton, basket weave, heavily embroidered in colored wool yarns.
12. Shirts and kilts: blue or black wool, basket weave.
13. Hair tie: cotton warp, red, floated patterns in green and white.

14. Garters: cotton or wool warp, red or black, floated patterns in black, white, red and green.
15. Wearing blanket: wool, soft loose weave, broad and fine stripes in many colors. (Worn with stripes in vertical position—shoulder blanket.)
16. Chief blanket: heavy wool blanket, tapestry weave, broad stripes of white, blue and red or orange, with design in center, and corners; worn horizontally.
17. Shoulder blanket: black and white plaid, twilled basket weave.

Household Textiles

18. Bed blanket: soft, loosely woven wool blanket, stripes in many colors, larger than wearing blanket.
19. Rabbit skin blanket: twining, or finger weaving.
20. Cotton and wool blankets: diamond weave.
21. Rugs: tapestry weave, Kachina design, or copy of Navajo.

Leather Work

22. Wedding boots: white doe skin, knee height, puttee tops, wound about the leg and tied.
23. Men's and women's low moccasins with tongues: buckskin dyed red, rawhide sole stitched with tendon.

Basketry (vegetable dyes and natural colors in many hues)

24. Oraibi wicker plaque (lump center).
25. Oraibi wicker shallow ceremonial plaque basket.
26. Oraibi wicker deep basket (modern forms).
27. Second Mesa coiled plaque.
28. Second Mesa coiled shallow ceremonial basket.
29. Second Mesa coiled deep basket (modern forms).

Utility Basketry, Natural Colors

30. Yucca winnowing basket.
31. Yucca deep basket.
32. Burden basket of wicker.
33. Piki tray, wicker.
34. Head cover for cradle board.
35. Cradle.
36. Matting door cover.
37. Grass bundle tied with yucca for door covers.

CHAPTER III

Cotton and Its History

COTTON IS A FIBER CLOTHING the seeds in the pods of certain shrubs and trees growing in tropical and semi-tropical countries and in various parts of western and southern United States where conditions are favorable for its culture.

The Hopi Indians originally grew their own cotton, native to parts of Arizona, a special species called *Gossypium hopi.** This cotton until recently was, and may be still, grown in small quantities to be used in ceremonies and hand spun. At the present time the Hopi use commercial cotton batting or usually cotton string for work in their textiles.

The color of cotton varies from deep yellow to white. The fiber differs in length, the long stapled being the most valued.

Cotton, unlike wool, requires special preparation for dyeing, as its fibers are water repellent. It is not washed with soap or yucca suds like wool, but must be boiled gently in plain water until thoroughly wetted and softened and the air bubbles pressed out.

There are two main methods of procedure, either of which may be followed in the dyeing of cotton.

Method 1

The first is that which is now used by the Hopi. Cotton is dyed and mordanted in one simple process; the mordanting agent being in the dye, into which the boiled spun cotton is immersed.

The method used by the Hopi is as follows:

After the spun cotton has been gently boiled, to soften and wet the fibers, it is lightly wrung or pressed out and immediately

* Whiting, 1939, p. 84.

6

immersed in the dye, which has already been mordanted. (See directions in recipes.) It is then boiled for a short period and set aside, in the dye, to soak for at least 24 hours. The one exception to this procedure will be found in the recipe for dyeing with natural indigo which is *not* boiled but soaked after the cotton is immersed in the dye.

Method 2

In the second method, the cotton is mordanted or prepared to receive the dye, previous to dyeing. These processes are varied and elaborate. The cotton is usually boiled or soaked in an astringent containing tannic acid, for which cotton has a natural affinity. This, in combination with other mordants and chemicals in the dyes, precipitates the coloring matter and fixes it in the fibers.

There are many variations in the mordanting and preparation of cotton for the dye bath, and in some cases the process is reversed and the cotton is soaked in an alum bath first and afterward boiled in an astringent solution of tannic acid.

Mordants

Tannic acid is contained in many plants and shrubs. (See Chapter V, mordants.) Stale urine, sheep manure, and the smoke of various plants and animal fibers have all been used as mordants from very ancient times all over the world.

CHAPTER IV

Wool and Its History

W OOL FIBERS are composed of a central cellular marrow called the medulla, which is incased in a substance composed of elongated conical cells, called the cortex, while the surface of the fiber is covered by rough epidermal scales.

These scales consist of a horny translucent substance, closely overlapping and varying in form according to the type of wool.

Reaction to moisture, heat and color

Wool fibers are extremely hydroscopic and when soaked in cold water, gradually soften and swell. When warm water or hot water is used, the process is accelerated. The epidermal scales open out and the fibers become gelatinous and temporarily lose their elasticity. In this state wool fibers show a greater affinity for dye stuffs. After washing and drying, therefore, wool should always be steeped in lukewarm water before immersing in a dye bath.

The above reactions may be studied under the microscope, when the physical changes, taking place in the fibers subjected to various treatments, can be clearly observed.

Wool, if subjected to high temperatures, either by long continued boiling or by dry heat, gradually decomposes.

Action of acids and alkalis

Wool is unaffected by dilute acids; in fact, it has a great affinity for them. But wool, being an animal fiber, is tendered and weakened by strong alkalis and when used in concentrated form they will completely dissolve it. Soaps containing caustic alkalis should never be used upon wool. Dilute alkalis are effective cleansing agents and may be used with care.

The best type of wool for native spinning and dyeing is the fleece of the "unimproved" or "old type" Navajo sheep.* This wool is long, loosely waved and comparatively free from lanoline or "wool fat." It is, therefore, easily scoured by the usual Indian method, with the pounded root of the yucca and cold or lukewarm water, instead of modern soap and hot water, which is essential for all "improved" or grease wools. In fact, this wool is so free of grease, and therefore contains so little dirt, that even today it is often not washed at all before dyeing, but is carefully selected and the dirt thoroughly shaken out. Formerly, this was a general custom among the Navajo, due to the scarcity of water.† However, if this yarn is to be used as white yarn and not dyed, or is to be dyed in indigo, it is always thoroughly scoured with yucca suds.

Wool to be used for dyeing and spinning is carefully selected from the shoulder and back of the fleece. This wool is usually the longest, finest and cleanest portion of the fleece. Stained wool from the lower and rear portion of the body of the sheep and the outside coarse, "hair-like" ends of the Navajo or "unimproved wools" are usually discarded. However, from the Hopi of Second Mesa, we have information that some weavers claim that the stained wool has a decided affinity for certain dyes and should be used without scouring as richer and more permanent shades can thus be produced. The writer has checked this information in the laboratory and finds it essentially correct.

How wool may be washed and dyed without shrinking

Extremes of heat and cold and violent changes of temperature have a tendency to shrink wool. Wool should be washed in lukewarm water at a temperature not higher than 100° F. and its rinse water should be of a similar temperature. In other words, it should not be subjected to violent changes of temperature during washing and scouring.

If this wool is to be dyed, the dye bath should also be lukewarm when the material is ready to be immersed. When the wool has been immersed in the lukewarm dye bath, it must be brought to a boil slowly and kept boiling at a low temperature.

When wool is to be dried after washing, or after it has been dyed, it should be dried in a warm room or outdoors in the sun.

* Colton, 1932.
† Amsden, 1934.

Ironing woolen material or subjecting it to freezing after washing will cause it to shrink badly.

Wool before dyeing: Wool that has been washed and allowed to dry before dyeing should be steeped or soaked in warm water for half an hour or so before immersing it in the dye bath. This will remove the air from the wool and soften it, so that it will take the dye more evenly.

Treatment of unwashed wool before dyeing: Wool that is to be used unwashed for dyeing, is carefully selected for its lack of grease and stain and is called "dry wool" because it feels dry to the touch, rather than cold and wet, like the grease wools. I have been informed that "dry wool" is usually chosen from the ewes.

After selection, this wool is carefully shaken out and it is then soaked for a few minutes in cold or lukewarm water, like dry washed wool, before immersing it in the dye bath.

Two native methods of cleaning wool

Washing wool with the suds of yucca root, narrow leaved or Hopi *mohu,* is practiced by both Navajo and Hopi.

The Navajo generally used cold water for this operation, while the Hopi seemed to prefer lukewarm water, saying that it makes better suds.

If the wool is very heavily laden with dirt and sand, it will first have the burs and sticks picked out and as much of the loose sand shaken free as possible. It will then be washed and steeped in plain water several times before the actual scouring begins.

Washing wool with white earth, or Hopi "Fullers earth,"* seems to have originated among the Hopi people, where this white earth is plentiful under their sandstone mesas.

However, I am told that certain Navajo also use the "white earth method" and that it is believed that they have copied it from the Hopi.

Washing and cleansing of wool: The Hopi, like the Navajo, has always used the root of the *Yucca angustifolia* or soap weed (several other types may be used for suds). It is prepared in the following manner.

The root of the yucca, which is about 18 inches long, is dug from the ground. It is a fibrous, tough, yellow substance, full of

* A colloidal alumnar sulphate.

a rather glutinous sap. These roots are pounded with a rock until the fibers are separated and torn apart.

A bowl of water is then warmed over the fire (or cold water is used) and the fibrous, pounded yucca root is placed in it and worked with the hands until a fine white suds is obtained. The yucca is then squeezed out and put away for future use. It may be used several times, after re-pounding, although the root is much more effective when fresh. It is used in cold water, but seems most effective in warm water (as the Hopi use it). It is slightly astringent.

Unimproved Navajo wool, washed once in yucca suds and then rinsed in warm water comes out a beautiful white, very light and fluffy.

Washing wool with white earth or Hopi "Fullers earth": The people of both Second and Third Mesas agree that this chalky white substance from the sandstone layers under the Mesas near their towns, acts as an excellent cleanser for both woolen and cotton stuffs. It is often used in place of yucca root. In fact, I am told that many women prefer it to yucca root. I have also been told that the Navajo adopted this cleansing method from the Hopi.

The wool or material to be washed, is carried to the spring and spread out on a flat rock nearby where it is sprinkled with the white powdered chalky earth. It is then thoroughly wet down with water and is kneaded and worked until the white earth is thoroughly mixed with the wool; it may or may not be rinsed. If it is to be spun and woven into a blanket, it probably will not be rinsed but merely dried and shaken out. Blankets, woolen dresses, etc., and also cotton goods, are washed in this way. This earth rinses out nicely and leaves the wool very white, soft and clean, and free of grease. This method has also been tested by the writer and the results on the "dry" or greaseless wool of the native sheep are excellent, but not as satisfactory on the "improved" wools, Rambouillet and crosses, which carry a heavy load of sticky grease.

The blood of the French Merino or Rambouillet has been extensively introduced by the government into the flocks of both Navajo and Hopi. These crosses have produced a type of wool entirely unsuitable for hand spinning and weaving. The fleece of merino types is heavily laden with a sticky grease called "wool fat" or lanoline, which renders it almost impossible for the Indian to scour properly with the primitive methods to which he is accustomed. This wool is extremely short, closely packed and sharply crimped. It carries an immense load of dirt embedded in the "wool fat."

Wool for hand spinning and weaving has requirements quite different from those for the machine. For the modern machine it is the fineness of the wool fiber that is of first importance, not the length, and a sharp crimp is not a disadvantage, as the machine is constructed to straighten this, and wools such as merino, heavily laden with grease, are easily cleaned by commercial methods.

Treatment of wool before dyeing

On this matter there seems to be a variety of opinions. An Oraibi informant tells us that the wool is always washed carefully with the suds of yucca root before being carded and spun, even brown wool, which is used instead of white, when a good black dye is desired. He has never seen unwashed wool dyed.

However, the same informant says that he has heard a rumor of wool being soaked in liquid sheep manure before dyeing. He thinks this may be something recent. ("Recent," among Indian peoples, may mean a matter of several hundred years.) He has also heard of rock salt being used as a mordant for dyes, but he does not know what particular dyes. This informant says cotton is never washed or wet before carding and spinning, because it mats up and this makes it hard to work with.

A Second Mesa informant says that wool sometimes is not washed at all, but only shaken out to free it of sand. He has seen this done particularly where the wool is to be dyed with "aniline dyes," especially the deep maroon red. This dyer believes that the dye "takes better" on the unwashed wool. Where wool is to be dyed with *hohoi'si* or *si:'ita* vegetable dyes, he says that it is first soaked in liquid sheep manure. All informants agree that wool is always carefully washed in yucca suds before dyeing it in indigo. The Second Mesa informant also states that cotton (perhaps after spinning), is almost always soaked in liquid sheep manure before dyeing and he thinks this may have been used as a mordant for wool also.

The Second Mesa informant says that when unwashed wool is dyed, the wool from the under parts of the animal is chosen, that which is stained by urine and manure in the corrals when the animal lies down.

The Oraibi informant does not know of this, although he states that this kind of wool is always used to smoke basketry and yarn.

It is probable that human urine, fermented, was used as a mordant in which to soak cotton before the introduction of domestic animals.

From these opinions, some idea of the latitude in native dyeing practices can be obtained.

The reasons for this are several, the principal being, that the Hopi have never had a "written language." Various clans and individuals use different methods.

It is interesting to note that all these opinions have precedent in early practices in other parts of the world. In India, cotton is mordanted with cow dung.

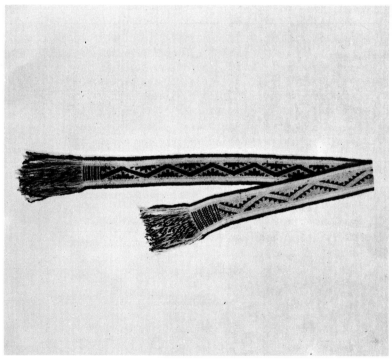

Belt from Oraibi.

CHAPTER V

Mordants, Chemicals and Measures

A MORDANT IS A CHEMICAL used to precipitate the active principal of the dye in the fiber. The mordant is said to fix or set the color and make the dye insoluble in water or water with neutral soaps. Mordants are used in two ways; either mixed with the dye or the textile is dipped in a mordant bath before or after the dye bath.

Common native Hopi mordants

1. Crude native alum from efflorescence of drying soil.
2. Limonite from Chinle or Mancos Shale.
3. Rock salt from Zuni Salt Lake or Grand Canyon.
4. Copper carbonate from copper ore from Verde Valley.
5. Cream-of-tarter, potassium tartrate.
6. Tannic acid from sumac *(Rhus trilobata)* berries, branches or leaves.
7. Lye made from wood ashes.
8. Human urine.
9. Sheep manure and water, filtered.
10. Smoke.
11. Iron tannate soot produced by burning pinyon gum with native ochre.

    Soluble in water 20.24%
    Total iron   5.68%
    Total sulphate   14.56%
12. "Potato Clay." This is a nickeliferous talc containing a small amount of aluminum.

Hopi Measures

Handfuls and double handfuls; their equivalent in grams and litres or millilitres, or cc.

Dry Measure: The measure by handfuls can be used for wool, cotton, indigo, whole plants and plant blossoms. These vary some-what, a handful of cotton, plants and plant blossoms being lighter in weight than wool or indigo. In measuring these materials in handfuls, fill the hands, stuff, and press tightly together.

	Measures
1 small double handful, wool	30-40 grams
1 large double handful, cotton	30-40 grams
4 double handfuls	160 grams
1 double handful	40 grams
2 double handfuls	80 grams
1 single handful	2.5 grams

Handfuls and double handfuls, their equivalent in litres or millilitres. These vary as much as 25 ml. This measure can be used for corn, beans, sunflower seed, sumac berries or other seeds —alum, salt, iron powder, copper carbonate, and powdered ochre.

	Measures
1 small single handful	25 ml.
1 large single handful	75 ml.
1 small double handful	100 ml.
1 large double handful	150 ml.
2 double handfuls	300 ml.
3 double handfuls	450 ml.
5 double handfuls	750 ml.
6 double handfuls	900 ml.

Liquid Measure: Quarts and cups — their equivalent in litres or millilitres, rough measure.

1 litre	1 quart or 4 cups
1½ litres	1 quart and 1 pint or 6 cups
2 litres	2 quarts or 8 cups
4 litres	4 quarts or 16 cups
150 ml.	½ cup
200 ml.	¾ cup
300 ml.	1-1/3 cups

Secondary Mordants — Smoking

The Hopi have always practiced smoking as a method of "setting the color" in various dyed materials.

It is used for basketry materials and for wool, also for cotton yarns to a lesser extent.

In the case of several dyes, smoking is relied upon to cause a complete chemical change in the color of the dyed materials, while in others, it serves only to intensify the shade and "set" the color.

Methods and materials used for the smoking of dyes: A fire of juniper wood is made, and allowed to burn down to embers. Dirty greasy wool is the material commonly used to place upon the charcoal, smothering the fire and thus causing a dense smoke. This wool is chosen from the underside and rear of the sheep and is soaked with urine and sheep manure, thus the thick yellow smoke produced contains a large amount of ammonia and other chemicals.

This smoke is very powerful as the writer has learned, inhalation of it having caused a severe attack of laryngitis.

At other times, corncobs are used, but the writer has not so far been able to ascertain whether this is always for a particular dye, or to take the place of the wool. Certainly they do not have the same chemical effect.

Smoking is sometimes done over an open fire, but in most cases, large storage jars, or tin wash boilers, are rigged up to contain the hot coals and wool, and so arranged that there is a draft at the bottom, and a method of suspending the material, whether basketry or yarn, over the smoking wool and coals. This contrivance is fitted with a top of some sort to control the smoke and to attain a maximum efficiency.

For the present experimenter, the "wash boiler" method, copied from an old lady in Oraibi, has proved most efficient.

The boiler has a row of holes about 2 or 3 inches from the bottom all around it, a wire rack for the material three-quarters of the way up, and a top which may be tilted in any direction to allow a good draft. The charcoal is produced in a fire nearby and transferred to the bottom of the boiler which is elevated from the ground upon stones.

Dirty wool, as described, is immediately placed over the live coals and produces a prodigious yellow smoke. The material at hand is then spread wet upon the wire rack, which is placed over the smoke, and the top is adjusted. Every few minutes the material is examined and turned about. If wool or cotton, the maximum effect will not be attained until the material has completely dried in the smoker.

However, no definite time can be given for smoking. Judgement and experience are required for the best results and the material is removed when the desired shade is obtained.

Dark brown or black wool is commonly used for the smoking of dark colors and white wool for light colors. This, however, the writer feels, has no real effect upon the results.

Soaps and Scouring Agents

Many vegetable dyes have a totally different reaction upon material washed with different scouring agents and soaps.

These scouring agents seem to act to some extent, as lesser mordants in themselves, causng the mordanted dyes to produce different shades upon materials scoured with the various agents.

The group of lavender, purple and carmine dyes, derived from starchy seeds, such as corn, beans and sunflower seed, are particularly influenced by the type of scouring agent used.

Upon wool washed with yucca suds, these dyes tend toward the red-purples, but on wool washed with a neutral soap such as Lux or Ivory, they develop a more bluish tone.

When this group of dyes is washed with soaps after dyeing, they almost all turn much more bluish.

The Hopi's present knowledge of complicated mordanting principles, which seem to be, with a few exceptions, tried more or less experimentally upon various plants in their present habitat, suggests that their art is very old, but that it has been transported in fairly recent times, perhaps hundreds of years, at least in part, to a new region with an unfamiliar flora.

It is felt that the present situation distinctly suggests a period of greater stabilization and a present deterioration of the dyer's art.

This may be partially due to the introduction of wool by the Spaniards in 1640, a new fiber to the Hopi, upon which many of the ancient dyes were not effective and, therefore, necessitating much additional experimentation.

CHAPTER VI

Preparation of Textiles for Dyeing

AFTER THE HOPI INDIAN has prepared his cotton or wool for dyeing, as described in the past few chapters, the material is ready for the dye bath. These dye baths are different for the different vegetable dyes, and in the following chapters the preparations of stock solutions are described and each stock solution may be further treated in different ways called recipes.

In making up these stock solutions and recipes the material is measured out. As the Indians do not have scales to weigh out ingredients or other measures they use single handfuls or double handfuls or cups to measure quantities. Cotton or wool have about the same specific gravity so that a single handful weighs about 25 grams and a double handful weighs about 40 grams. For a fluid measure the Indian uses teacups; four cups equal about a quart or a litre.

The classification of stock solutions and recipes is based on color (a) from the red to gold and red-brown, (b) gold to yellow, (c) blue, (d) purple, and (e) black.

In some cases the dyed material has been tested for fading or for washing with soap.

Interesting ceremonial customs are connected with the gathering of dye plants as well as many strange superstitions.

Before a man goes out into the country to gather plants for his dyes, he makes a prayer to each particular kind of plant.

If a woman is pregnant, she must be very careful not to "run in" on a man or woman who is doing dye work, for if she does, the color will not take on the material. The only thing that she can do to help, if this has happened, is to apologize to the dyer and then spit into the dye pot, when everything will at once be well.

On the other hand, if a pregnant woman is doing some dye work herself and a neighbor comes in, it will spoil the dyer's work. But worst of all, if a man has been in a house where someone has died or has helped to bury a friend, should he then happen in on a dyer at work, it will cause all his dyed material to fade. There is nothing that can be done about this.

In comparing Navajo dye plants used by Mrs. Bryan* with the Hopi plants and dye materials, only three plants are used by the Hopi and not by the Navajo. There are also three plants used by both Hopi and Navajo and twenty-four plants are mentioned as used by Mrs. Bryan that were not mentioned by the Hopi informants.

Since the Hopi and Navajo Indians occupy similar environments, one would naturally expect them to use the same resources, but in regard to dye plants the Hopi do not use many of those used by Mrs. Bryan, a Navajo.

* Bryan and Young, 1940.

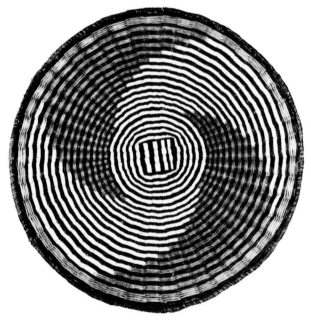

Whirlwind plaque from Third Mesa.

COLOR RANGE CHART
Hopi Dye Plants (12 color groups)

Colors

reds	purple corn—(Hopi *koko'ma*) produces	carmine-pink
carmines	Maerz and Paul, 6-4-H, purple	carmine-reds
madders		raspberry-red
maroons		maroon-reds
		deep maroon-red
	sunflower, black-seeded	deep maroon
		purple and deep
		lavender
vermilion	*hohoi'si (Thelesperma megapotamicum)*	vermilion
and	*si:'ta (Thelesperma subnudum)*	vermilion
apricots		
pink	*saya'vi (Rumex hymenosepalus)*	apricot-pink
rust-reds	*hohoi'si (Thelesperma megapotamicum)*	rust and
Indian-reds	*si:'ta (Thelesperma subnudum)*	Indian-reds
orange-golds	*hohoi'si* and *si:'ta*	red-orange
and	*saya'vi (Rumex hymenosepalus)*	deep gold
burnt orange	*hohoi'si (Thelesperma megapotamicum)*	burnt orange
yellows	*saya'vi (Rumex hymenosepalus)*	deep gold
and	*tu'i'tsma (Pectis angustifolia)*	shades of gold
golds	*hohoi'si* and *si:'ta*	deep golds
	siva'pi yellows (tall variety)	shades of
		bright gold
	siva'pi blossoms (Recipe No. 4)	greenish-gold
	goldenrod *(Solidago* sp.)	brilliant gold
lemon	*siva'pi* yellows, mature blossoms and	
yellow	stems	greenish-yellows
	siva'pi, second size	greenish-yellow
	siva'pi (tallest variety)	pale yellow
ochre yellow	ochre or mineral yellows	brown-earth
		yellows
greens	*siva'pi* indigo (Recipe No. 2)	dark green
	siva'pi indigo (Recipe No. 1)	deep green
	siva'pi, immature plants	pale green
	siva'pi, stems and leaves	pale green
	siva'pi blossoms (2nd size plants)	yellow-greens
	siva'pi blossoms	gold-green
blues	indigo blue (trade article)	deep blue
	koko'ma (purple corn) blue	lavender-blue
	sunflower seed	medium blue
	blue kidney bean	purple-blue
		and blue

purples and lavenders	*koko'ma,* purple corn	bright purple
	blue kidney bean	purples and lavender-blue
	sunflower seed (black)	dark lavender
	sunflower seed	dark purple

tans and browns	*koko'ma,* purple corn	tan
	koko'ma, purple corn (cobs)	red-brown
	mountain mahogany bark	deep rust brown

| blacks | No. 1 — iron tannate from mixture of pinyon gum, ochre and black seeded sunflower | black |
| | No. 2 — iron tannate from pinyon gum, ochre and sumac leaves | black |

PLANTS USED FOR DYES IN THIS BOOK

tu'i'tsma	Fetid marigold	*(Pectis angustifolia)*
hohoi'si		*(Thelesperma megapotamicum)*
si:'ta	Navajo-tea	*(Thelesperma subnudum)*
putci'vi	Mountain mahogany	*(Cercocarpus breviflorus var. eximius)*
siva'pi	Rabbit brush	*(Chrysothamnus sp.)*
na'palnga	Golden rod	*(Solidago sp.)*
saya'vi	Canaigre	*(Rumex hymenosepalus)*
tupenmori	Blue kidney bean	*(Phaseolus vulgaris)*
'a:'gaw'u	Sunflower	*(Helianthus sp.)*
koko'ma	Purple corn	*(Zea mays amylacea)*
su:'vi	Sumac	*(Rhus trilobata)*

CHAPTER VII

Reds and Golds and Red-browns

tu'i'tsma (Pectis angustifolia)

Tu'ı'tsma is an inconspicuous plant with fine composite yellow blossoms. When mature, it is about 4 inches high and has a delicious "lemon verbena" odor. It grows in the sand dunes near the Hopi mesas. The whole plant is gathered while in blossom and used at once or dried for future use.*

This plant is not as highly valued as the thelespermas, as it is capable of producing one color only, an old gold shade, somewhat similar to that produced by *si:'ta* before smoking.

Its color is not materially altered by smoking or the use of acids or strong alkalis. We have no record of its use by the Navajo or other tribes and therefore, believe that it is peculiar to the Hopi alone.

Tu'i'tsma is equally effective on basketry, cotton or wool. It is used today upon all three. It is used upon the Third Mesa wicker material but not upon the Second Mesa yucca basketry material.

Its preparation is simple. The plants are packed into a kettle and well covered with water. This is brought slowly to a boil and kept boiling gently for several hours, refilling when necessary. It is then removed from the fire and strained through a cloth and squeezed out thoroughly. The resulting liquid is a clear yellow-brown.

Ground or melted native alum is then added to the liquid, which at once turns a rich, opaque old gold.

The mixture is replaced on the fire and allowed to boil for a few minutes. It is then ready to receive the material to be dyed.

* Whiting, 1939, p. 97.

For the dyeing of basketry material, the dye bath may be brought to the boiling point, but not allowed to boil after the material has been immersed. The dye is placed in a receptacle sufficiently long to accommodate the prepared *siva'pi* (rabbit brush) stems, either loose or tied in small bundles. There should be sufficient dye to cover the material and the pan should be rocked at intervals and the bundles turned to insure the dye taking evenly upon all the material.

The material is removed when it has attained the desired shade, and is placed damp in the smoker. Sometimes it is smoked and then dipped again and this process may be repeated several times to increase the depth of the shade.

First Mesa coiled basket.

TU'I'TSMA GOLD

Stock Dye No. 1*

Use blossoming, whole plants, 4 inches high.

4 double handfuls (100 grams) of plants. Place in 4-quart kettle and cover with water, 16 cups (4 litres).

Bring to boil slowly. Boil 1-2 hours gently. Refill when necessary.

Reduce to 8 cups (2 litres).

Strain through cotton cloth; squeeze out well.

Result: Clear, yellow-brown liquid.

* A stock dye is a dye solution before mordanting.

Recipe No. 1   For wool and cotton

TU'I'TSMA GOLD

tu'i'tsma (Pectis angustifolia)

Use Stock Dye No. 1.

Mordanting: Take 1 small double handful (100 ml.) of native alum. Pour into hot iron frying pan. Sprinkle with little water, melt down and pour into dye, which at once turns to rich, deep, opaque gold. This plant yields a large amount of rich color.

Material added: Into 8 cups (2 litres) of dye immerse 1 double handful (30-40 grams) of wool washed in yucca suds or cotton soaked in hot water.

Treatment in dye: Boil 1-2 hours.

After treatment: Soak overnight. Remove, wring slightly and dry. Rinse thoroughly.

Result: Wool — a clear, light, old gold; cotton — boiled 1 hour in dye; result: fine, deep, old gold. Soaked overnight, results the same.

(Maerz and Paul, 12-L-5, Light stone L)*

* Color determinations have been made for some recipes, based on the Maerz and Paul system of color identification.

Recipe No. 2   For wool and cotton

TU'I'TSMA GOLD
tu'i'tsma (Pectis angustifolia)

Use Stock Dye No. 1.

Mordanting: Add to this dye 1 small double handful (100 ml.) of ground native alum. Liquid at once turns rich, opaque gold.

Material added: Into 8 cups (2 litres) of this dye, immerse 1 double handful (30-40 grams) of unwashed wool or cotton which has been soaked 24 hours in strong liquid sheep manure. Remove, wring slightly and place damp in dye.

Treatment in dye: Boil 1 hour or more.

After treatment: Remove, wring slightly. Immerse damp in urine and work for a few minutes. Wring and dry. Rinse thoroughly.

Result: Brilliant old gold on both wool and cotton; cotton slightly darker. Urine both enriches color appreciably and adds to permanency.
(Maerz and Paul, wool, 11-L-7, Yelow Ochre P; cotton, 13-L-9, Chipmunk.)

Recipe No. 3   For wool and cotton

TU'I'TSMA GOLD
tu'i'tsma (Pectis angustifolia)

Use Stock Dye No. 1.

Mordanting: Add to this dye 1 small double handful (100 ml.) of ground native alum. Liquid at once turns rich, opaque gold.

Material added: Into 8 cups (2 litres) of this dye immerse 1 double handful (30-40 grams) of unwashed natural wool, dampened, or cotton that has been soaked in boiling water.

Treatment in dye: Bring to a boil and simmer gently for 1 hour or more.

After treatment: Remove, wring slightly. Immerse damp in urine bath and work for a few minutes. Rinse in several waters. Wring lightly and dry.

Result: Good shade of old gold on wool; poor on cotton.
(Maerz and Paul, 12-L-6, Tennis)

Additional experiment tried: Test: Washed in Lux soap — good, light gold; then run through urine bath — deep gold.

Recipe No. 4   For wool and cotton
TU'I'TSMA GOLD
tu'i'tsma (Pectis angustifolia)

Material: Tu'i'tsma, mature blossoming plants 4 inches high. 100
    grams plants. 15 ml. water.

Mordanting: Boil 3 hours and strain; liquid yellow-brown. Put 1
    double handful (50 grams) of native alum in hot iron frying
    pan, sprinkle a little water on alum; melt down alum at once
    and pour into dye. Dye turns a deep old gold.

Material added: Put in wool, yucca washed; cotton, plain boiled.

Treatment in dye: Boil cotton in dye 1 hour. Boil wool in dye 2
    hours and soak overnight; rinse wool.

Result: Wool, clear, light, old gold. Lime water and ammonia do
    not alter this color. Cotton, a fine, permanent, old gold, washed.

GOLDS AND REDS
hohoi'si* (Thelesperma megapotamicum)
si:'ta* (Thelesperma subnudum)

Habitat, character and properties as dyes

These two little plants, closely related, are of great interest. Of all the Hopi dye plants, they are capable of producing the richest and most permanent shades.

The Hopi value them highly and apparently they are used only by them, as we have no evidence that either of these plants are used by the Navajo or other tribes today. However, many well preserved Puebloan specimens of prehistoric cotton cloth from northern Arizona and the Verde Valley, closely match the shades produced today from these plants, so that we strongly feel that these dyes have indeed come a long way, and are very ancient favorites.

The thelespermas, *hohoi'si* and *si:'ta*, are both inconspicuous annual plants growing in sandy soil in certain restricted locations, particularly around the base of the Hopi mesas, at an altitude of about 4,500 feet. *Hohoi'si* may attain a height of 2 feet while *si:'ta* averages about 6 inches.

When these small plants first appear, they are difficult to differentiate. They yield the richest dye if gathered before the first rains, when only several inches high. If rain falls at this stage and the plants are examined immediately after the shower, it will be seen that there is a small blot of color in the sand, at the base of the young plants. Therefore, the careful Hopi weaver will gather the young plants before the rains, when they contain the maximum sap, and dry them for future use.

The small daisy-like composite flowers of the mature *hohoi'si* are also very effective as dye and are gathered and dried for use. The mature plants of both the thelespermas may be used, but the dye content is not as rich as in either the immature plants or the flowers.

The minute clusters of composite flowers of the *si:'ta* cannot conveniently be separated from the small plants which never attain a height of more than 6 inches. Therefore, the whole of this plant, flowers and all, is used in this case.

* Whiting, 1939, p. 98.

Both thelespermas yield rich shades ranging from deep old gold to brilliant orange-red, depending upon the stage in which the plant is gathered and the mordanting and treatment of the dye.

Both these dyes are sensitive to strong alkalis and their colors may be completely altered by the ammonia in the smoke of burn-ing wool, or by immersion in a bath of stale urine (ammonia).

These dyes are equally effective upon cotton and wool or upon basketry material, and they are used today upon all three.

Both wicker and yucca basketry materials are dyed with these plants.

Preparation and Dyeing Process

The preparation of these dyes is simple. Either the green or dried plants or flowers are packed into a kettle and covered with a generous quantity of water. This is brought slowly to a boil and boiled gently for an hour or so. More water is added as necessary.

When it is removed from the fire, the liquid is strained through a cloth or fine strainer and the plants well squeezed out.

The result is a very rich, rather cloudy, red-brown liquid. Ground native alum is added to this, turning it a fine, opaque Indian red.

Replace the dye on the stove and bring it to a boil. When it has boiled for a few minutes, remove and let it cool slightly. It is now ready to receive the prepared damp wool or cotton.

(1) For light shades of old gold and tan, wool and cotton should not be smoked after dyeing.

(2) For deep shades of red-brown, both cotton and wool are smoked as described in the chapter on this process.

(3) To produce very intense shades of orange-red or vermilion, the dyed material, when removed from the dye pot and wrung out, may be placed in a solution of stale urine and worked in this for a few minutes. A very brilliant shade results. (See Recipe No. 2.)

When removed from the urine bath, the material should be thoroughly rinsed in several waters, and dried in the sun. The Hopi practice of smoking both these thelesperma dyes is used today, however, we have no authority, other than a strong suspicion, founded upon usage and colors which we have seen produced, that the Hopi made use of the urine bath for this plant, although it is used in many other cases.*

For the dyeing of basketry material see page 22.

---

* Used by Navajo (Bryan and Young, 1940, p. 69).

GOLDS AND REDS
hohoi'si (Thelesperma megapotamicum)

Stock Dye No. 1

Use blossoms.

1 large double handful (40 grams) *hohoi'si* blossoms, 8 cups (2 litres) of water. Bring to a boil slowly; boil gently 2 hours, adding water when necessary. Reduce to 6 cups (1½ litres). Strain through cotton cloth. Squeeze out.

Result: Clear, rich, dark brown liquid. These blossoms yield a very rich dye.

Stock Dye No. 2

Use mature, whole plants, without blossoms.

2 double handfuls (80 grams) *hohoi'si* plants. Place in 4-quart kettle and cover with 12 cups (2 litres) of water. Bring to boil slowly. Boil gently 4 hours, adding water as necessary. Reduce to 8 cups (2 litres). Strain through cotton cloth. Squeeze out.

Result: A dirty, brown-colored liquid.

Recipe No. 1   For wool and cotton
OLD GOLD
hohoi'si (Thelesperma megapotamicum)

Use Stock Dye No. 1.

Mordanting: Add to this dye 1 small double handful (100 ml.) of ground native alum. Dye at once turns opaque, yellow-brown.

Material added: Into 6 cups (1½ litres) of this dye, immerse 1 double handful (30-40 grams) of wool washed in yucca suds and rinsed, or cotton soaked in hot water.

Treatment in dye: Bring to boil slowly and boil 1-2 hours.

After treatment: Remove and wring lightly and dry. Rinse thoroughly.

Result: Wool, good, deep, old gold; cotton, somewhat redder.

Variation: Cotton may also be brought to boil in dye and then soaked for 24 hours.

Variations of Recipe No. 1

> (1) Smoked and then run through diluted ammonia water.
> Result: Good orange-gold or red-orange.
>
> (2) Wool washed in Lux or Ivory soap. Finished by smoking.
> Result: Good orange-gold.
>
> (3) Wool, Lux or Ivory washed. Finished by rinsing in diluted ammonia.
> Result: Clear orange-red.
>
> (4) Wool, Lux or Ivory washed. Finished by rinsing in diluted lye water.
> Result: Dull old gold.
>
> (5) Wool, Lux or Ivory washed.
> Result: Clear old gold.

Recipe No. 2   For wool

HOHOI'SI VERMILION – SI:'TA VERMILION
(Thelesperma megapotamicum) – *(Thelesperma subnudum)*

Use recipes for *hohoi'si* and *si:'ta* yellow.

Mordanting: Dye yarn in *hohoi'si* or *si:'ta* yellow; rinse thoroughly. Now take urine which has been aged for 1 week and gives off a strong odor of ammonia, place this in a jar.

Material added: Immerse yellow *hohoi'si* or *si:'ta* dyed yarn into the stale urine.

Result: Yarn at once turns an intense shade of orange-scarlet. A very fine color. Dry yarn in shade in the open air.

Remarks: Aged urine when exposed to the air for any length of time, loses strength and this will cause the dyed gold yarn to take a longer time to turn vermilion in the urine bath.

Recipe No. 3   For wool and cotton

ORANGE-RED
hohoi'si (Thelesperma megapotamicum)

Use Stock Dye No. 1 and Recipe No. 1.

When thelesperma gold material has been thoroughly rinsed, it is placed at once in stale urine, sufficient to completely cover material. It immediately turns a brilliant, rich orange-red. A very fine color. Allow it to steep at least 5 minutes. Remove and rinse several times in hot water and dry in sun.

Result: A very fine brilliant orange-red. It is also effective on cotton, but does not produce such a brilliant red.

Washing test: Wool, quite fast to washing; cotton, same.

(Maerz and Paul, 4-J-12, 4-K-12, Totem)

Recipe No. 4   For wool and cotton
RED-BROWN
hohoi'si (Thelesperma megapotamicum)

Use Stock Dye No. 1 and Recipe No. 3.

Smoking: When thelsperma gold *(hohoi'si)* material is removed
from dye, and lightly wrung out, it is ready to be placed damp
in smoker. Smoke about 1 hour, or until material is dry or
desired shade of red-brown is reached.

Result: Wool, a fine Indian red; cotton, poor.
(Maerz and Paul, 5-B-12, Cacao Brown)

Recipe No. 5   For wool and cotton
PALE GOLD
hohoi'si (Thelesperma megapotamicum)

Use Stock Dye No. 2.

Mordanting: Add to this 1 double handful (100 ml.) of native
alum, previously melted in a hot iron pan, with a little water.
Pour into dye liquid.

Material added: Into 4 cups (1 litre) immerse 1 single handful
(25 grams) of wool washed in yucca suds and rinsed, or cotton
soaked in hot water.

Treatment in dye: Bring to boil slowly and boil gently 3-4 hours
in the dye.

After treatment: Remove, wring slightly, dry and rinse thoroughly.

Result: Wool, a very pale gold; cotton, a poor, dirty gold. Cotton
much better when brought to a boil, then soaked overnight
for 24 hours.

(Maerz and Paul, 12-L-4, Sulphin Yellow R.)

Recipe No. 6   For wool
BURNT ORANGE
hohoi'si (Thelesperma megapotamicum)

Use Stock Dye No. 2.

Add to 4 cups (1 litre) of water, 25 ml. of rock salt and immerse 1 single handful (25 grams) of wool. Boil 1 hour.

Remove, rinse and immerse again in Stock Dye No. 2. Boil 2 hours.

Result: Good, strong, gold color.

Variation: Run this wool through a bath of stale urine, rinse well and dry in sun.

Result: A fine, clear, burnt orange.

(Maerz and Paul, 13-A-12, Titian Gold)

Recipe No. 7   For wool and cotton
HOHOI'SI GOLD
hohoi'si (Thelesperma megapotamicum)

Use mature *hohoi'si*, no blossoms.

Boil 2 double handfuls of plant in ¾ cup (200 ml.) of water 4 hours.

Add water from time to time as it evaporates. Liquid is a dirty brown color.

Mordanting: Add 50 grams of alum dissolved in water in pan to strained liquid.

Material added: Into 2 lots of this liquid, put Navajo wool washed in yucca, and wool boiled in rock salt. One lot, yucca washed, wool *very pale.*

Result: This dye turns orange with ammonia, like small *hohoi'si* plants and blossoms. Lot boiled in salt, then in dye, much stronger color. Smoked, turns brilliant Indian red. Cotton from both processes, pale and dull brown.

Recipe No. 8   For wool
HOHOI'SI GOLD
hohoi'si (Thelesperma megapotamicum)
Use blossoms.
1 large handful (50 grams) blossoms.
8 cups (2 litres) water.
Bring to boil slowly and boil 2 hours.
Strain; liquor resulting is a clear dark brown.

Mordanting: Add 40 grams ground native alum; dye turns opaque yellow-brown.

Material added: Immerse Navajo wool washed in yucca and rinsed. Boil for 2 hours. Rinse and dry.

Result: A nice, golden orange.

Recipe No. 9   For wool, cotton and basketry
HOHOI'SI RED
hohoi'si (Thelesperma megapotamicum)

Material added: Immerse this wool, (resulting from Recipe No. 8) into pure stale urine, 1 week old, smelling of ammonia.

Result: Hohoi'si yellow dyed wool at once turns an intense orange-scarlet. A wonderful color! *Si:'ta* will do the same. *Siva'pis* are not much affected by urine. Urine seems to lose strength when exposed to air and wool takes longer to turn red. When wool is finally washed twice in hot water it does not lose any color. Fresh urine will also change cotton or basket material to a nice red-orange. It does not work as rapidly and the result is not such a brilliant red.

For basketry

GOLDS AND REDS
hohoi'si or *si:'ta* (*Thelesperma* sp.)

Any of the recipes given under Thelesperma Golds and Reds may be used for basketry material, both yucca and peeled rabbit brush stems and quite possibly, other basketry fibers. These dyes are strong and the shades intense, they take readily both on animal and vegetable fibers.

Dyeing

In a receptacle long enough to accommodate the length of the material (10-12 inches) the mordanted dye is allowed to cool until nearly lukewarm. The stems or yucca strips, are immersed in this dye bath, either loose or in bundles tied lightly. The vessel is gently agitated at intervals and the bundles are turned so that the dye will take evenly on the material. The dye may be reheated during the process but never brought to a boil. The Navajo also use these plants.*

Smoking

If a bright orange or deep red-brown shade is desired, it will be smoked while still damp. The bundles of dyed basketry material should be placed in the smoker and smoked until the desired intensity or shade is obtained. It may be necessary to re-dip the material in the dye, which has been reheated several times during the smoking process. (See Chapter V.)

* Bryan and Young, 1940.

Dye experiment   For wool only
RED-BROWN
putci'vi (Cercocarpus breviflorus var. eximius)

Take 1 double handful of the bark of the root of the mountain mahogany. Place in a kettle and cover well with water. Boil this for about 2 hours or until liquid is a clear, deep, red-brown. Remove from fire and strain off liquid.

Mordanting: Take 1 handful native alum and boil down.

Material added: Pour off clear liquid, replace on fire and immerse yarn that has been soaked in warm water previously.

Treatment in dye: Boil yarn ½-¾ hour. Now remove yarn, wring lightly and place in dye. Boil gently for at least 2 hours.

After treatment: Remove yarn and wring lightly to dispose of extra dye.

Result: A good, strong, red-brown.

CHAPTER VIII

Yellows and Golds

siva'pi or Rabbit Brush *(Chrysothamnus sp.)*

Habitat, character and properties as a dye

THERE ARE MANY SPECIES of this handsome, well-known plant throughout the Southwest. They vary in size from 1 foot to 5 feet in height and all bear composite yellow blossoms. They are found in the high desert and foothill country. Four species are used in these recipes.

Because this plant is widely distributed geographically and its use as a dye is known to the Navajo* as well as the Hopi and possibly to other Indian peoples of the Southwest, it is felt that this could be classed as one of the older native dye stuffs. The Hopi use at least three or four varieties of this perennial plant.

Mature flowers are gathered when in their prime and either used at once or dried and stored in quantities for use during the coming winter.

If yellow-green is desired, immature blossoms are used or the pale green stems of the plant itself will produce a delicate shade of green.

Mature blossoms from the different varieties produce a series of shades, from lemon-yellow to a deep, golden color.

Siva'pi dye is equally effective upon cotton, wool, or basketry materials. It is in use among the Hopi today, upon all three. We have no recent record of its modern use upon cotton, as there is very little cotton dyeing done, except for ceremonial purposes.

The preparation of this dye is simple. It has one phase only, the

* Bryan and Young, 1940, p. 56.

alkaline. Native alum, aluminum sulphate, is the mordant in general use. This color appears unaffected by acids and is not sensitive to temperature changes.

Smoking or the "urine bath," only very slightly intensify the shade, though it is thought that either treatment has a tendency to render the color more permanent.

Exposure to sunlight or intense light, over a period of years, causes this dye to turn slightly brownish.

To dye wool

Wool should be placed damp in the warm mordanted dye bath and brought to a boil slowly and boiled gently for several hours, or until the desired shade is obtained.

To dye cotton

Cotton, like most vegetable fibers, takes the dye better when soaked, rather than boiled for a long period. However, it should first be placed damp in the mordanted dye bath and brought slowly to a boil and kept boiling for a few minutes, then it should be removed, set aside and soaked for 24 hours.

Basketry material, Third Mesa type only

Siva'pi (rabbit brush) stems for the Third Mesa wicker basketry are peeled and steeped in this dye. For this purpose, the mordanted dye is allowed to cool until nearly lukewarm, in a receptacle long enough to accommodate the length of the material (10-12 inches).

The stems are immersed in this, either loose or tied lightly in bundles, and the vessel is gently rocked at intervals, and the bundles turned to dye the material evenly.

Siva'pi dye may be considered as a "fairly fast" dye. It is permanent to washing but loses color when exposed to light over a long period — turns brown.

Smoking

For an intense shade of gold: while still damp, bundles of dyed basketry material may be placed in the smoker and smoked until the desired shade is attained, in about ½ hour or until material dries. It may be necessary to re-dip in dye several times during the smoking process. (See Chapter V.)

Object: wicker basketry plaque, whirlwind design

Maker: Mary George

Date: 1978

Diameter: 11 inches

Dyes: blue — indigo
             red — *hohoi 'si, Thelesperma megapotamicum*
             yellow — *siva 'pi, Chrysothamnus* sp.
             green — indigo; and *siva 'pi, Chrysothamnus* sp.
             black — *'a: 'gaw'u, Helianthus* sp.

Comment: The amount of dye was varied to obtain the two shades of blue.

MNA Catalogue Number: E8157

Object: coiled basketry plaque, *Angwusnasomtaka* (Crow Mother Kachina) design

Maker: Martha Laban

Date: 1973

Diameter: 14½ inches

Dyes: red — *si: 'ta, Thelesperma subnudum*
black — *'a: 'gaw'u, Helianthus* sp.

MNA Catalogue Number: E6245

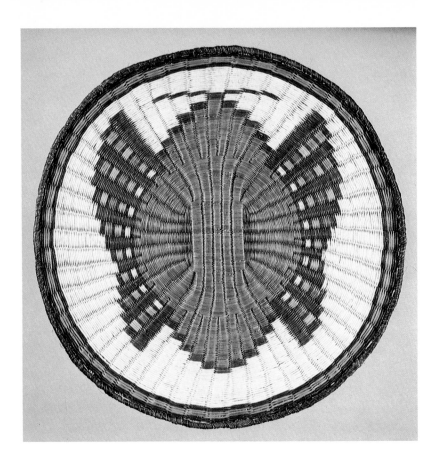

Object: wicker basketry plaque, butterfly design

Maker: Eva Hoyungwa

Date: 1973

Diameter: 14 inches

Dyes: purple — *koko 'ma, Zea mays amylacea*
              green — indigo; and *siva 'pi, Chrysothamnus* sp.
              brown — *hohoi 'si, Thelesperma megapotamicum*
              blue — indigo
              yellow — *siva 'pi, Chrysothamnus* sp.
              black — commercial

MNA Catalogue Number: E6201

Object: wicker basketry doll cradleboard

Maker: Susie Herman

Date: 1934

Length: 20¾ inches

Dyes: orange — *hohoi 'si*, *Thelesperma megapotamicum*
           yellow — *siva 'pi*, *Chrysothamnus* sp.
           green — indigo and *siva 'pi*, *Chrysothamnus* sp.
           black — *'a: 'gaw'u*, *Helianthus* sp.

Comment: The dyes are definitely vegetable, but identifications are tentative.

MNA Catalogue Number: E323

Object: coiled basket, corn design

Maker: Gladys Kagenvema

Date: 1973

Diameter: 12 inches

Dyes: red — *hohoi 'si, Thelesperma megapotamicum*
               black — *'a: 'gaw'u, Helianthus* sp.

MNA Catalogue Number: E6209

Object: blanket

Maker: Elmer Sequoptewa

Date: 1977

Length: 57 inches

Dyes: blue — indigo
             green — indigo; and *siva 'pi,*
                     Chrysothamnus sp.
             black — *'a 'gaw'u, Helianthus* sp.

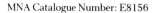

Comment: The black dye was applied to a natural black wool to insure a
             deep and even color.

MNA Catalogue Number: E8156

Object:	man's shirt
Maker:	Talashongniwa
Date:	1938
Length:	31 inches
Dyes:	blue/black — indigo
Comment:	The dye was probably applied to a natural black or brown wool, resulting in a shade so deep it appears black.

MNA Catalogue Number: E361

Object: woman's dress

Maker: Charlie Polingyoma

Date: ca. 1939

Length: 52 inches

Dyes: blue — indigo

MNA Catalogue Number: E2625

Stock Dye No. 1

SIVA'PI YELLOW
siva'pi (Chrysothamnus sp.)

Use tall variety — flowers large and decidedly yellow.
2 double handfuls (80 grams) of blossoms. Add 8 cups (2
litres) of water, or sufficient to cover well. Bring to boil slowly.
Boil 1-2 hours gently and reduce to 6 cups (1½ litres) of dye.
Strain through a cotton cloth and squeeze out well.

Result: A clear, dark amber liquid. This liquid should be strained
off through a cloth and well squeezed out. The resulting liquid
or stock dye should now be replaced upon the stove and
ground or melted native alum added to the clear liquor, when
the dye will immediately turn an opaque, greenish-yellow.
After this has been boiled for a few minutes and slightly
cooled, it will be ready to receive the damp wool or cotton to
be dyed. The pan may then be set upon the stove and reheated, but not boiled. If an intense shade is desired, remove
and smoke while damp.

Stock Dye No. 2

1 double handful (40 grams) *siva'pi* blossoms. 3 cups (½ litre
stale urine. 3 cups (½ litre) water or enough to cover blossoms
well. Bring to a boil slowly. Boil 1 hour. Strain through cotton
cloth and squeeze out well.

Result: Dark brown liquid.

Stock Dye No. 3

SIVA'PI YELLOW
siva'pi (Chrysothamnus sp.)

Use stems.

Break *siva'pi* stems and pack into 4-quart kettle. Cover with water, about 16 cups (4 litres). Boil slowly for 2 hours, adding water when necessary. Reduce liquid to 8 cups (2 litres). Strain through cloth.

Result: Pale, yellowish-green liquid.

Stock Dye No. 4

Use blossoms, tallest variety; flowers are long and pale, straw color; yellow blossom tip not prominent.

1 double handful (40 grams) *siva'pi* blossoms. 8 cups (2 litres) of water or sufficient to cover well. Bring to a boil slowly. Boil 1-2 hours gently and reduce to 6 cups (1½ litres). Strain through cloth — squeeze out.

Result: Clear, brownish-yellow liquid.

YELLOWS AND GOLDS
siva'pi (Chrysothamnus sp.)

Use Stock Dye No. 1.

To dye wool: Wool should be placed damp in the warm mordanted dye bath and brought to a boil slowly and boiled gently for several hours, or until the desired shade is obtained. If a more intense shade is desired, remove the wool and smoke while still damp.

To dye cotton: Cotton, like most vegetable fibers, takes the dye best when soaked in the dye bath. It should be placed, damp, in the mordanted dye and brought slowly to a boil and boiled gently for a few minutes only. It should then be set aside and soaked for 12 hours.

Recipe No. 1   For wool, cotton and basketry

SIVA'PI YELLOW
siva'pi (Chrysothamnus sp.)

Use Stock Dye No. 1.

Add to this liquid 1 double handful (100 ml.) of ground native alum. Liquid at once turns an opaque, greenish-yellow.

Material added: Into 6 cups (1½ litres) of dye, immerse 1 double handful (40 grams) of wool washed in yucca suds or cotton soaked in hot water.

Treatment in dye: Bring to a boil slowly and boil 1-2 hours.

After treatment: Remove material, wring slightly and dry. After drying, rinse thoroughly.

Result: Wool, good, brilliant yellow; cotton, good; basketry fibers, good.

Variation: For cotton, better results are obtained in most cases, by immersing in a hot dye bath, bringing to boil, then setting aside to soak for 12 hours.

Recipe No. 2   For wool and cotton

SIVA'PI YELLOW
siva'pi (Chrysothamnus sp.)

Use Stock Dye No. 1 and Recipe No. 1.

Material added: Into 6 cups (1½ litres) of Stock Dye No. 1 immerse 1 double handful (40 grams) of wool washed in yucca suds or cotton soaked in hot water.

Treatment in dye: Bring to boil slowly and boil 1-2 hours.

After treatment: Remove material and wring slightly. Dry and rinse thoroughly.

Result: Wool, good, greenish-yellow; cotton, better results are obtained by immersing in hot dye bath, bringing to boil and then soaking for 12 hours, instead of boiling in dye.

(Maerz and Paul, 12-L-3, Pyrite Yellow R.)

Recipe No. 3   For wool and cotton
SIVA'PI YELLOW
siva'pi (Chrysothamnus sp.)

Use Stock Dye No. 4.

Mordanting: Add to this liquid 1 double handful (100 ml.) of ground native alum. Liquid turns a light, opaque, yellowish-green.

Material added: Into 8 cups (2 litres) of dye, immerse 1 double handful (30-40 grams) of wool washed in yucca suds or cotton soaked in hot water.

Treatment in dye: Boil 2 to 3 hours.

After treatment: Remove, wring slightly and dry; then rinse thoroughly.

Result: Wool, a nice pale yellow; cotton, dull. Better results obtained on cotton immersed in hot dye, brought to boil and soaked 12 hours. Result: color similar.

(Maerz and Paul, 11-L-2, Pyrethrum Yellow)

Recipe No. 4   For wool and cotton
SIVA'PI YELLOW
siva'pi (Chrysothamnus sp.)

Use Stock Dye No. 4.

Mordanting: Add to this 1 double handful (100 ml.) of ground native alum. Liquid at once turns an opaque, brownish-yellow.

Material added: Into 6 cups (1½ litres) of dye immerse 1 double handful (40 grams) of wool washed in yucca suds or cotton soaked in hot water.

Treatment in dye: Bring to boil slowly and boil 1-2 hours.

After treatment: Remove material, wring slightly and dry. Rinse thoroughly.

Result: Wool, a fine, golden-green; cotton, color rather dull.

Soaking: Cotton brought to boil only and then soaked in dye for 12 hours gives a much brighter shade.
(Maerz and Paul, cotton; 11-K-3, Colonial Yellow)

Smoking: Smoking cotton and wool intensifies color slightly and renders material more permanent.

Recipe No. 5   For wool
SIVA'PI YELLOW
siva'pi (Chrysothamnus sp.)

Use stems, tall variety.

Boil stems 2 hours in 8 cups (2 litres) water. Resulting liquid, pale greenish.

Mordanting: Add 40 grams of native alum. Resulting liquid light, opaque, yellow-green.

Material added: Wash wool in yucca; immerse and boil for 2 hours.

Result: Pale yellow, washes satisfactorily.

Recipe No. 6   For wool and cotton
SIVA'PI YELLOW
siva'pi (Chrysothamnus sp.)

Use blossoms; large blossoms with yellow tip in end of blossom; possibly the tallest variety.

Put 2 double handfuls blossoms in 8 cups (2 litres) water. Boil 2 hours. Strain liquid which is dull, yellowish-brown.

Mordanting: Add 40 grams native alum; turns opaque, yellow-brown.

Material added: Put in wool washed in yucca and boil 2 hours. Dry and wash wool. Boil cotton in water, immerse in hot dye and soak for 4 hours.

Result: Wool, a fine greenish, canary yellow; cotton, bright yellow.

Recipe No. 7   For wool and cotton
SIVA'PI YELLOW
siva'pi (Chrysothamnus sp.)

Smoking: Smoking dyed cotton and wool slightly intensifies color and renders shades more permanent. Place, while damp, in a smoker and smoke until material dries or the desired color is obtained. Remove and rinse thoroughly in lukewarm water.

Result: Wool, a good, brilliant yellow; cotton, similar to wool.

Recipe No. 8   For wool and cotton
SIVA'PI YELLOW
siva'pi (Chrysothamnus sp.)

Siva'pi blossoms — they are the largest type of blossoms and a very pale color. The blossom tip is not as bright yellow as the other varieties. Put 2 double handfuls blossoms in ¾ cup (200 ml.) of water. Boil 4 hours and strain. This produces a pale brownish liquid.

Mordanting: Add 40 grams native alum. Liquid turns opaque, greenish-yellow.

Material added: Wash Navajo wool in yucca and rinse. Immerse in dye. It assumes a pale canary color. Boil 2 hours. Soak cotton in dye; do not boil.

Result: A fine, canary yellow. Smoking intensifies color. Cotton rather dull.

YELLOWS AND GOLDS
na'palnga or Golden Rod *(Solidago sp.)*

Habitat, character and properties as a dye

There are many species of golden rod, large and small, growing at different altitudes and under many conditions all over the United States.

It bears heads of small composite flowers of a golden color, which produce a rich dye. This dye is similar in character and in its reactions to the *siva'pi* yellow dyes.

This dye was used by early American (white) dyers and weavers, and there is also a possibility that it was used by the Hopi, but this cannot be stated positively.

Golden rod makes an excellent dye for cotton, wool and basketry material. (For basketry, see recipe for *siva'pi* yellows.)

Stock Dye No. 1

YELLOWS AND GOLDS
na'palnga (Solidago sp.)

Use blossoms.

2 double handfuls (30 grams) of blossoms to 8 cups (2 litres) of water, or sufficient to cover well. Bring to boil slowly. Boil gently 1-2 hours and reduce to 6 cups (1½ litres). Strain through cotton cloth. Squeeze out well.

Result: Clear, golden-brown liquid.

Recipe No. 1   For wool and cotton
YELLOWS AND GOLDS
na'palnga (Solidago sp.)

Use Stock Dye No. 1.

Mordanting: Add to this liquid 1 double handful of ground native alum. Liquid at once turns an opaque, greenish-yellow.

Material added: Into 6 cups (1½ litres) of dye, immerse 1 double handful (40 grams) of wool washed in yucca suds or cotton soaked in hot water.

Treatment in dye: Bring to boil slowly and simmer gently 1-2 hours.

After treatment: Remove material, wring slightly and dry; then rinse thoroughly.

Result: Wool and cotton, a very brilliant, canary yellow. These shades are more intense than any other yellows. Turns slightly more reddish in time, but is fast.

(Maerz and Paul, 11-L-1, Chartreuse)

Recipe No. 2   For wool and cotton
YELLOWS AND GOLDS
na'palnga (Solidago sp.)

Use Stock Dye No. 1 and Recipe No. 1.

When material has been removed from dye, place in boiling soapy water (Ivory Flakes) and simmer a few minutes.

After treatment: Remove, rinse, wring slightly and dry.

Result: A very rich, deep, gold color.

(Maerz and Paul, 11-L-5, Lime Yellow)

Stock Dye No. 1

MINERAL YELLOW

Take 1 large double handful of Mancos Shale containing limonite found near Polacca, and cover with 4 cups (1 litre) of water. Crush lumps of earth with fingers and stir the mass every few minutes, then let it settle. A clear liquid will rise to the top as the earth settles and will gradually turn a deep, clear, claret-red color. Allow this to stand overnight. Decant and use as it is, or put through filter paper.

Result: A perfectly clear claret-red liquid. No odor nor reaction to changes in temperature. Sand left after settling is a very fine, gray material.

Recipe No. 1   For wool

MINERAL YELLOW

Use Stock Dye No. 1.

Preparation of material: Take wool that has been washed in yucca suds and rinse.

Treatment in dye: Place in warm dye and stand aside to soak. Soak 24 hours.

After treatment: Remove, wring slightly and dry. Rinse thoroughly.

Result: A good yellow-ochre color.

Washing test: Very fast.

APRICOTS AND GOLDS
saya'vi or Canaigre *(Rumex hymenosepalus)*

Habitat, character and properties as a dye

The desert dock grows in the beds of sandy washes and on flats and it is occasionally cultivated by certain tribes. It has a long carrot-like root. This is gathered and used to produce a fine gold or orange-apricot dye. The root may be used while fresh, or, dried and stored. It yields an abundance of rich brown dye which seems equally effective on wool or cotton.

Note: Also used by Navajo (Bryan and Young, 1940, p. 28).

Basketry

It is said to be a good dye for basketry materials also. The writer has not experimented with these fibers, but recommends doing so.

Stock Dye No. 1

APRICOTS AND GOLDS
saya'vi (Rumex hymenosepalus)

Take the long carrot-like root of the desert dock and brush off sand. Put about 6 of these roots into a large kettle and cover with cold water; let them soak overnight. In the morning they will be soft and must be carefully peeled; do not remove more of the skin than necessary. Cut them up into small pieces and replace in the water in which they have soaked overnight. Put on the stove and bring to boil slowly. Boil gently several hours. Remove and strain through a cloth and squeeze out liquor.

Result: A clear, dark brown liquor.

Recipe No. 1   For wool and cotton
APRICOTS AND GOLDS
saya'vi (Rumex hymenosepalus)

Use Stock Dye No. 1.

Mordanting: This dye is a "natural dye" and contains within itself both dye and mordant, probably tannin. Therefore, it needs no additional mordanting.

Material added: To 6 cups (1½ litres) of this dye add 1 double handful (30-40 grams) of wool washed in yucca suds and rinsed or cotton soaked in hot water.

Treatment in dye: Immerse in dye, bring to boil slowly and boil 1-2 hours.

After treatment: Remove, wring slightly and dry, then rinse thoroughly.

Result: A fine, old gold.

Washing test: Very fast.

    (Maerz and Paul, 13-L-7, Tinsel Deep Stone)

Variation: When alum is added to this dye, a more brilliant yellow results.

    (Maerz and Paul, 12-L-5, Sulphin Yellow)

Recipe No. 2   For wool and cotton
APRICOT
saya'vi (Rumex hymenosepalus)

Use Stock Dye No. 1 and Recipe No. 1.

After treatment: When material has been removed from dye and wrung slightly, place it while damp in warm stale urine. Work it in the urine for about 10 minutes. Remove and rinse thoroughly several times in hot water and dry in the sun.

Result: A fine shade of apricot.

    (Maerz and Paul, 12-A-11, Maya)

Washing test: Very fast.

Smoked: Similar results may be obtained by smoking the material when removed from the dye bath. This color is not as pink as when not smoked.

CHAPTER IX

Blues

Indigo blue — natural or vegetable indigo

THE CULTIVATION AND THE USE of indigo is very ancient both in India, the East Indies, in Central America and Mexico.

Indigo is grown principally in India and Indonesia today where it has been used for centuries for the dyeing of cotton fabrics and other vegetable fibers.

From prehistoric times it was grown and used as a textile dye in Central America. There is strong evidence that it was a valuable article of trade, which, traveling from tribe to tribe through Mexico, finally reached our own prehistoric peoples of the south-western United States.

It is certain that up to fifty years ago, impure lump indigo was still traded into the pueblos of the Rio Grande Valley. With the discovery of synthetic indigo, commercial cultivation of the plant ceased in Central America and Mexico and the supply from this ancient source was cut off.

Indigo produces the finest shades of blue (slightly greenish) on cotton, wool and other vegetable and animal fibers. It is absolutely permanent.

There are many methods of dyeing with indigo. One of the oldest of these, is the Cold Indigo Vat prepared with stale urine. This has long been in use in many parts of the world. This method is still used today by the Hopi, Navajo and other Pueblo peoples of the Southwest.*

Of all the dyes used by the Hopi, indigo is the most precious to him. It is the sacred color of the sky. The Hopi name, *saqwa*, is

* Indigo is not mentioned by Bryan and Young, 1940, for the Navajo.

used to mean blue, of the sky, the precious turquoise, and the blue of flowers, birds and butterflies. Next to turquoise, it is the most precious thing that he might possess.

Synthetic indigo can be purchased from Du Pont but it is not recommended for the Hopi because it requires the use of sodium hydroxide which is dangerous to have around a home with children running about. It does not require the use of urine as a reducing agent because other chemicals are used for reduction. It is easy to use but is not recommended for a household industry.

Recipe No. 1   For wool, cotton and basketry

INDIGO BLUE
(lump indigo*)

Preparation of urine — collect human urine in a large pottery storage jar, keeping the top carefully sealed. Allow to stand in a warm room for some days or until it gives off a strong odor of ammonia. It is now ready for use. 2 gallons of stale urine in 4 gallon jar. About 1 large double handful (270 grams) of indigo lumps. Tie indigo in cloth, dip in liquid and beat out color against the side of the jar as it dissolves. Then allow indigo sack to remain in liquid. Stand this jar overnight in a warm room, either covered with a close top or with cloth tied tightly over the top.

Preparation of material: Next day take 2 hanks of spun yarn, cotton or wool, or about 2 pounds that has been thoroughly washed in yucca suds before spinning.

Material added: Wet this thoroughly in cold water. If wool soak, if cotton wring out gently and place in the indigo, which now appears to be covered with a greenish scum.

Treatment in dye: Stir down and thoroughly soak yarn in dye by manipulation with sticks. Prepare 6 small sticks just the width of the jar top and wedge them in on top of the floating yarn, thus keeping the material below the surface of the dye. Let this stand for 4 days — open the jar each day and thoroughly "handle" the wool with a pair of sticks. If this is not done, the wool will turn greenish wherever the air touches it and will not take the dye evenly.

After treatment: On the fourth day, remove the wool and wring it out lightly. The wool will appear green when first exposed to the air. It should be hung at once in the open air where oxidation will take place and it will shortly turn a fine, rich, dark blue. Allow it to dry thoroughly then rinse in a succession of warm waters until wool ceases to yield color, when it should again be hung in the air and dried.
Cotton as well as Third Mesa basketry material may be dyed in the same manner and results are equally good.

* Lump indigo can be purchased through the Museum of Northern Arizona, Flagstaff, Arizona.

Result: Wool and cotton both a fine, deep blue. For a light, bright
blue, two days soaking will be found sufficient.

Washing test: Fast.

Light test: Fast.

(Maerz and Paul, wool, 39-A-12; cotton, 38-H-6, Harbor Blue)

BLUES
tupénmori or Blue Kidney Bean *(Phaseolus vulgaris)*

Habitat, character and properties as a dye

This bean is said to be of a very ancient type. It is cultivated
today by the Hopi. It is valued particularly as a source of blue dye.

It is a solid blue-black bean of the kidney type with a powdery
bloom on the surface, ends are square to rounded and the size is
variable, usually quite small.

Like sunflower seed and corn, the bean has a starchy interior
and the dye is in the outer skin of the shell. Therefore, care must
be taken not to allow this bean to boil *after the skin has cracked
open,* or the color of the dye will be spoiled by the starchy interior.

This bean produces a blue dye effective on cotton and on wicker
basketry fibers. It cannot be used on wool.

Colors range from blues to purple-blues.

Stock Dye No. 1   For cotton and basketry

BLUES
tupénmori (Phaseolus vulgaris)

3 double handfuls (450 ml.) of beans. 10 cups (2½ litres)
of water. Bring to boil slowly. Boil gently for 20 minutes to ½
hour, or until skin of beans begins to crack open. Strain through
cloth.

Result: Dirty, brownish-blue liquid.

Recipe No. 1   For cotton and basketry
PURPLE-BLUE
tupénmori (Phaseolus vulgaris)

Use Stock Dye No. 1.

Mordanting: Add to the liquid stock dye 1 small double handful
(100 ml.) of ground native alum. Liquid instantly turns an
intense, deep purple. Boil down to 6 cups (1½ litres) of dye.

Material added: To 6 cups (1½ litres) of this dye add 1 double
handful (30-40 grams) of cotton or cotton yarn which has been
soaked 24-48 hours in a preparation of ground copper carbonate
and water. (See Purple Corn Dye, Recipe No. 6.) Remove and
press out water lightly.

Treatment in dye: Immerse in hot dye bath and soak several hours,
or until a good shade is procured.

After treatment: Remove and dry without wringing. Rinse thoroughly and press out lightly.

Result: A fine, clear, purple-blue.
(Maerz and Paul, 43-A-5)

Recipe No. 2   For cotton and basketry
BLUE-PURPLE
tupénmori (Phaseolus vulgaris)

Use Stock Dye No. 1 and Recipe No. 1.

Preparation of material: Substitute cotton washed in Lux or Ivory
soap, rinse, then soak.

Treatment in dye: Immerse in dye and soak several hours.

After treatment: Remove, without wringing. Rinse thoroughly *after
drying* and re-dry.

Result: Good, deep blue-purple. Dulled by rinsing.

Recipe No. 3   For cotton and basketry
PURPLE-BLUE
tupénmori (Phaseolus vulgaris)

Use Stock Dye No. 1 and Recipe No. 1.

Preparation of material: Substitute spun cotton boiled and soaked in plain water, squeeze out lightly and immerse in dye.

Treatment in dye: Soak several hours.

After treatment: Remove from dye. Dry without wringing. Rinse thoroughly after drying and re-dry.

Result: Color similar to cotton soaked in copper carbonate, a fine, clear, purple-blue. This is good for basketry material also. (Maerz and Paul, 43-B-7, Ontario Violet)

For basketry

BLUES
tupénmori (Phaseolus vulgaris)

This dye is a good basketry dye, especially effective on the peeled stems of the rabbit brush, *(siva'pi)*, used in wicker basketry. Any of the recipes given may be used, with the possible exception of Recipe No. 1.

Dyeing

For this purpose, the mordanted dye is allowed to cool until nearly lukewarm, in a receptacle long enough to accommodate the length of the material (10-12 inches).

The stems are immersed in this, either loose or tied lightly in bundles, and the bundles are turned so that the material will be evenly dyed.

Smoking

For strong shades of blue:

While still damp, bundles of dyed basketry material should be placed in the smoker and smoked until the desired shade is obtained. It may be necessary to re-dip in dye several times during the smoking process. (See Chapter V.)

Bean Blue Dip

Dip basketry material in Bean Blue Dye. Have wet sand ready on a canvas and put the blue dyed basketry material in the sand and work it about.

Result: a brilliant blue.

CHAPTER X

Blues and Purples, Carmine Reds, Maroons

Stock Dye No. 1

'a:'qaw'u or Sunflower Seed *(Helianthus* sp.)

Sunflower seed — 2 double handfuls (300 ml.). Water — 8 cups (2 litres). Bring to boil slowly. Boil gently not more than ½ hour, or until seeds split open. Strain through cloth.

Result: Deep maroon liquid.

Recipe No. 1   For wool and cotton
PURPLE
'a:'qaw'u (Helianthus sp.)

Use Stock Dye No. 1.

Mordanting: Add to this liquid 1 small double handful (100 ml.) of ground native alum. Dye turns a deep, royal purple.

Material added: To 6 cups (1½ litres) of this dye, add 1 double handful (40 grams) of wool washed in yucca suds and rinsed or cotton soaked in hot water.

Treatment in dye: Immerse in dye. Bring to boil slowly. Boil gently about ½ hour and remove from fire.

After treatment: Allow material to soak in dye for 24 hours. Remove material, wring slightly, dry and rinse thoroughly after drying.

Result: Wool, a dull, dark lavender; cotton, a fine, deep purple.

Washing test: Wool not fast.

Light test: Cotton turns bluish.

(Maerz and Paul, wool, 47-C-7; cotton, 47-E-8)

Recipe No. 2   For wool
BLUE
'a:'qaw'u   (Helianthus sp.)
Use Stock Dye No. 1.

Mordanting: Add to this liquid 1 small double handful (100 ml.) of
  ground native alum. Dye turns a deep, royal purple.

Material added: To 6 cups (1½ litres) of this dye, add 1 double
  handful (40 grams) of wool which has been washed and
  boiled ½ hour in Lux or Ivory soap and rinsed.

Treatment in dye: Immerse in dye and bring to boil slowly. Boil
  gently 1-2 hours.

After treatment: Remove, wring slightly, and dry; rinse thoroughly.

Result: Wool, a good blue.

Washing test: Not fast to soap.

For basketry material
BLUES AND PURPLES
'a:'qaw'u   (Helianthus sp.)

These recipes are effective on wicker basketry (peeled stems of
siva'pi or rabbit brush). Fine blues and purples can be produced.

Dyeing

The mordanted dye is allowed to cool until nearly lukewarm, in
a receptacle long and deep enough to accommodate the length
of the material (10-12 inches). The stems are immersed in this
dye bath either loose or tied lightly in bundles. The vessel is gently
agitated at intervals and the bundles turned, so that the dye will
take evenly on the material.

Smoking

The smoking of sunflower seed blues and red-purples, causes
the blues to darken and dull and the red-purples to turn a cold
blue. If this is desired, while still damp, bundles of dyed basketry
material can be placed in the smoker and smoked until the desired
shade is obtained. (See Chapter V.)

koko'ma or PURPLE CORN
(Zea mays amylacea)

History

The Hopi Indians believe this corn to be one of the oldest original types of corn which they possess.

Formerly a Hopi used great care in planting his corn of different colors in separate plots, not because he realized that the varieties would cross, but from some obscure feeling that each of the sacred colors should have its own ground.

The main types of corn recognized by the Hopi are those colors which stand for the "six directions" of the Hopi compass. These read from left to right, and are represented on the sacred altars thus:

> Northeast — yellow corn
> Northwest — blue corn
> Southwest — red corn
> Southeast — white corn
> Upward — purple corn
> Downward — sweet or flint corn

With the exception of the sweet and flint corns, the other color varieties are all flour corns. The Hopi claim that all these varieties of corn are their own from ancient times. Other varieties of lesser importance recognized, are popcorn, blue spotted corn, gray-blue corn and lavender corn. The people realize today that all varieties of corn cross, and that this accounts for the many mixtures of flint, dent and flour corns and their myriad color varieties.

Its character — properties as a dye

The coloring matter extracted from *koko'ma* or purple corn is used today for a number of purposes by the Hopi. A young boy's first ceremonial kilt of hand spun cotton is dyed a soft lavender-blue in this dye. This kilt is not boiled in the dye but soaked.

Corn dye is used as a textile dye for both cotton and wool and also for basketry material on Third Mesa. As a paint with a base of white clay, it is used on ceremonial wooden objects and as a body paint. It seems most probable that at one time *koko'ma* dye was more extensively used for cotton textiles and later possibly for wool, but at present only a faint trace of its former uses upon textiles can be discovered.

Proceeding with this theory, and because actual recipes for

further uses of this dye may be unearthed at any time, the writer has made a series of experiments, the results of which are given under the recipes for *koko'ma* dyes. In carrying out these experiments both the native mordants derived from local plants and minerals, and the common modern soaps and household cleaners have been used. No chemicals to which the Indian would not have had access, either in ancient or in modern times, have been introduced.

The best type of this corn to use as a dye is the deep purple or almost black type. The cob must also be purple for the best results. The purple cob is also used for dye and produces a lighter shade. The dyes produced from this corn are either a deep, royal purple or carmine-red, depending upon the mordanting. If the corn is white, a strong dye cannot be made from the kernels.

Two main colors may be derived from the kernels of the purple corn and from these a great variety of shades may be produced by variations in handling and the use of the mordants.

Stock Dye No. 1

The shelled purple corn is placed in an enamel vessel and well covered with cold water. This is brought slowly to a boil and allowed to boil gently not longer than ½ hour. As it begins to heat, a purple-red color is given off. This deepens with boiling to a fine, clear, carmine-red.

This dye is very sensitive to changes of temperature and extremely tricky, especially before the mordant has been added. It should be boiled gently for not more than ½ hour, or *until the grains begin to crack open,* when it must be removed at once and the liquor strained off through a fine sieve or cloth. The result is a fine, clear, deep carmine-red liquor.

If the corn is allowed to boil too long after the grains have cracked, the dye rapidly turns brownish. If this dye is chilled and reheated or boiled at a high temperature, it will also lose color. Therefore, when the liquor has been strained off, it should be kept warm and used as soon as possible.

This dye stock may now be treated in four ways:

Method 1. It may have the concentrated liquor of sumac berries added to it. This causes the dye to brighten in color.

Method 2. Ground native alum may be added. This causes the carmine dye to turn at once, a deep, fine purple. But, if this dye is subjected to much heat, or to boiling more than five or ten minutes, it will gradually revert toward the red.

Method 3. The stock dye may have some sumac berry liquor added to it, and in a few minutes a small amount of ground native alum. In this case the alum, added after the sumac berry liquor, only brightens the dye and does not cause it to turn purple. After boiling this dye for more than ½ hour, it may lose brilliancy. The addition of more sumac berry liquor will revive it. After this, it would seem that the dye has reached an equilibrium and will now stand boiling for any length of time without changing color. It will stand for days and can be reheated without undergoing any noticeable change.

Method 4. The stock dye may have ground native alum added to it, as in method 2, when it turns a deep purple .This dye may then be boiled for several hours, when it gradually loses the purple color and reverts to a carmine-red. In this state it seems stable and no longer sensitive to temperature changes. Unwashed wool and cotton, mordanted in weak lye water, and dyed in this dye, becomes a fine, carmine-pink. This color is fast to rinsing in warm water and even to soap, but will not stand high temperatures which cause it to lose color and turn gray-blue.

Summary of Various Methods

Method 1. Both wool and cotton can be dyed with this method; wool, a good maroon that is fairly fast and cotton a good, carmine-pink, either by boiling or, preferably, by soaking. However, this color is not fast on cotton, either to washing or to light. Even rinsing causes it to turn bluish.

Method 2. Both wool and cotton can be dyed by this method and good shades of purple, lavender, and slate blue can be produced, depending upon the method of washing and preparing the wool and cotton, (see recipes). Though several of these shades are in the "fairly fast" class, they all have a tendency to turn toward blue when washed and to lose color from prolonged exposure to light.

Method 3. Both wool and cotton can be dyed by this method and the beautiful shades of raspberry-red and maroon produced on wool are the most permanent to washing, of this group, especially when they are smoked after dyeing. Prolonged exposure to light turns them brownish, although fine shades of pink, to lustrous maroon, can be produced on cotton, they are not fast to washing, as they at once turn blue, even when rinsed. The same is the case when material is smoked. Light also fades them badly.

Method 4. Both wool and cotton can be dyed by this method and fine shades of carmine-pink produced. These are quite fast to rinsing and even to washing with soap and warm water, but will not stand high temperatures. They turn a dirty bluish color. The same is the case when material is smoked.

Conclusions: While corn dye can be made to produce many fine soft shades on cotton, wool and basketry, ranging through purples and slate blues to carmine-reds, maroons, browns and tans, none of these can be considered in the permanent class. In both washing and light tests they lose color.

For basketry

CARMINE AND RED-BROWN
koko'ma (Zea mays amylacea)

Third Mesa wicker basketry material can be dyed with any of the following methods.

The dye is placed in a container of sufficient length to accommodate the material. The *siva'pi* (rabbit brush) stems are then immersed in the lukewarm mordanted dye, either loose or in bundles, and soaked.

The vessel is rocked at intervals and the bundles turned, so that the material will dye evenly.

Occasionally it is carefully reheated during the process.

The carmine and red-brown shades from this dye are not smoked, as it causes them to change color.

Stock Dye No. 1

CARMINE
koko'ma (Zea mays amylacea)

Corn — 3 double handfuls (450 grams). Water — 10 cups (2½ litres). Bring to boil slowly. Boil gently ¾ hour or until kernels begin to crack open. Strain through cloth.

Result: Deep, carmine-red liquid.

Stock Dye No. 2

KOKO'MA BROWN
koko'ma (Zea mays amylacea)

Break corncobs that are a deep, red-purple in small sections and half fill a 6-quart kettle. Cover with 16 cups (4 litres) of water. Bring to boil slowly. Boil gently for 1-2 hours. Boil down to ½ quantity. Strain through cloth.

Result: Deep, carmine-red liquid (not quite as intense as that from corn kernels).

Stock Dye No. 3

KOKO'MA RED
koko'ma (Zea mays amylacea)

Corn — 5 double handfuls (750 grams). Water — 16 cups (4 litres). Bring to boil slowly. Boil gently ¾ hour or until kernels begin to crack open. Strain through cloth.

Result: Deep, carmine-red liquid.

Recipe No. 1   For wool and cotton
KOKO'MA PURPLE
koko'ma (Zea mays amylacea)

Use Stock Dye No. 1.

Mordanting: dye and mordant one process. Add to this, 1 small
   double handful (100 grams) of ground native alum. Liquid
   at once turns deep purple. Boil down to 6 cups (1½ litres).

Material added: To about 6 cups (1½ litres) of this dye add 1
   double handful (30-40 grams) of wool washed with a neutral
   soap or cotton boiled in plain water.

Treatment in dye: Immerse in dye, bring to boiling point slowly and
   boil 15-20 minutes. Remove from fire.

After treatment: Set aside and soak for 48 hours. Remove from dye,
   wring lightly and dry, then rinse thoroughly after drying.

Result: Wool, deep purple; cotton, deep purple.

Washing test: Wool, fairly fast to rinsing; cotton, same.

Light test: Does not fade.
   (Maerz and Paul, 46-F-6)

Test No. 1 (alkali)
   Use Stock Dye No. 1 and Recipe No. 1.

Preparation of material: Substitute wool washed and boiled in Lux
   soap for ½ hour.

After treatment: Set aside and soak for 24 hours, or 48 hours, if
   purple is desired.

Result: Wool, good lavender; smoked, slightly darker; cotton, same.

Washing test: Fairly fast, slightly lighter. More bluish, good.

Test No. 2 (alkali acid)
   Use Stock Dye No. 1 and Recipe No. 1.

Preparation of material: Wool washed in Lux soap and then boiled
   in sumac berry liquid before dyeing.

Result: Saddens* purple toward brown.

---

* Sadden — make dark or dull.

Recipe No. 2   For wool and cotton
KOKO'MA PURPLE
koko'ma (Zea mays amylacea)
Use Stock Dye No. 1 and Recipe No. 1.

Preparation of material: Use wool washed in yucca suds and rinsed; weak alkali.

Treatment in dye: Immerse in dye. Boil ½ hour.

After treatment: Remove from stove, set aside and soak 24 hours.

Result: Wool, fair lavender; cotton, fine purple.

Washing test: Wool, fairly fast, paler, more bluish; cotton, not fast, turns blue.

(Maerz and Paul, 45-D-8, 46-H-9, 47-E-7)

Recipe No. 3   For wool and cotton
KOKO'MA PURPLE
koko'ma (Zea mays amylacea)
Use Stock Dye No. 1 and Recipe No. 1.

Preparation of material: Use carefully selected wool, with the dirt well shaken out. Soak in warm lye water for ½ hour (alkalizer). Wring slightly and immerse in dye. Do not wash.

Result: Wool, a fine, deep purple; cotton, a fine, deep, reddish-purple.

Washing test: Wool, fast — turns slightly bluish; cotton, fast — loses reddish tinge.

(Maerz and Paul, wool, 47-E-8; cotton, 46-K-8)

Recipe No. 4   For wool
KOKO'MA PURPLE
koko'ma (Zea mays amylacea)

Use Stock Dye No. 1.

Wool — 2 lots

Mordanting: Lot No. 1, washed in yucca suds and rinsed. (Cleanser
and mordant in one.)

Lot No. 2, washed in Lux soap and rinsed. (Weak alkaline
dyes.)

Treatment in dye: Immerse these two lots of wool into two separate
hot dye baths and bring slowly to boil. Boil gently for 15
minutes.

After treatment: Remove dye containers from stove and allow wool
to remain in dye bath for 24 hours. Remove, press out surplus
dye, shake out and dry.

Result: Brilliant purple.

Washing test: Wool, fairly fast to rinsing in plain water.

Recipe No. 5   For wool and cotton

KOKO'MA PURPLE
koko'ma (Zea mays amylacea)

Use Stock Dye No. 1.

Mordanting (before dyeing): Take 1 small handful (100 grams) of ground native alum and dissolve in about 2 litres of warm water.

Material added: Place 1 double handful (30-40 grams) spun yarn or loose wool or cotton in warm alum water, bring to boil slowly and boil gently about 15 or 20 minutes. Remove the mordanted yarn, wring lightly and place at once in warm dye bath, about 6 cups (1½ litres).

The dye bath: Bring to boil and boil gently for about ½ hour. Stir and turn the yarn about in the dye bath.

After treatment: Remove from fire, press out surplus dye, shake out material and dry, then rinse thoroughly.

Result: Wool, a brilliant purple; cotton, same.

Washing test: Neither wool nor cotton lose color when rinsed in plain water. (Washed with Ivory soap, turns slightly bluish.) (Maerz and Paul, 44-B-6)

Recipe No. 6   For cotton

CLOUD LAVENDER, CEREMONIAL DYE
koko'ma (Zea mays amylacea)

Use Stock Dye No. 1.

Mordanting: Add to this 1 small double handful (100 grams) of ground native alum. Liquid at once turns deep purple. Allow this dye, about 8 cups (2 litres) to heat slowly but do not bring to boil.

Preparation of material: Grind copper carbonate to powder on stone mortar; 1 double handful (75 ml.) to about 1½ gallons of water. Stand aside in jar. Soak cotton ceremonial kilt or spun cotton for 2-4 days in this mixture. Remove, dry and shake out.

Treatment in dye: Rinse material and place wet in 8 cups (2 litres) of dye and soak ½ hour or until cotton assumes desired shade. Cotton takes deep purple after 1 hour soaking.

After treatment: Remove, wring slightly and dry. Rinse thoroughly.

Result: Cotton, fine lavender.

Washing test: Not fast. Washed with soap turns light blue.

Test No. 1

Use Stock Dye No. 1 and Recipe No. 6.

Preparation of material: Substitute wool or cotton that has been washed in Lux soap and rinsed and then boiled ½ hour in alum water.

Treatment in dye: Immerse in dye, bring to boiling point slowly and boil 1 hour.

Result: Wool, a good, dark purple; cotton, same.

Washing test: Wool turns slightly bluish; cotton turns more purple.

Test No. 2

Use Stock Dye No. 1 and Recipe No. 6.

Material added: Substitute wool or cotton washed in Lux soap and rinsed.

Treatment in dye: Soak in dye 48 hours.

Result: Wool, a good, bright purple; cotton, same.

Washing test: Wool and cotton, not fast, lose color.

Recipe No. 7   For wool, cotton and basketry

KOKO'MA CARMINE-PINK
koko'ma (Zea mays amylacea)

Use Stock Dye No. 1 or No. 3.

Mordanting: Add to this, 1 small double handful (100 ml.) of ground native alum. Liquid at once turns deep purple (alkaline). Now boil this gently for 1-2 hours and it will gradually lose its purple color and turn back toward the original carmine-red color (acid). Boil down to about 1/3 quantity of liquid or until the dye thickens slightly and becomes a very rich carmine color (acid). Now add enough warm water to bring the quantity up to 6 cups (1½ litres).

Material added: To this dye add 1 double handful (30-40 grams) of wool or cotton washed in yucca suds and soaked for ½ hour and then rinsed.

Treatment in dye: Immerse in dye, bring to boiling point slowly and boil gently for 1 hour.

After treatment: Set aside and soak overnight. Remove from dye, wring slightly and dry. Rinse thoroughly after drying.

Result: Wool, a fine, carmine-pink; cotton, the same. (The addition of an alkali to the purple corn turns it a blue-purple; while acid turns it a carmine-red.)

Recipe No. 8   For cotton

KOKO'MA CARMINE-PINK
koko'ma (Zea mays amylacea)

Use Stock Dye No. 1 (acid dye).

Mordanting: Take 1 handful (20-25 grams) of sumac berries to
1-1/3 cups (300 ml.) of water and boil berries ½ hour, or they
may be soaked 24 hours. Strain berries through cloth and
squeeze out juice. Replace on fire and boil down to 6 cups
(1½ litres).

Material added: Take cotton yarn or loose cotton and soak 24 hours
in sumac berry acid, dry, then rinse.

Treatment in dye: Immerse cotton in bath of (acid) carmine dye
(Stock Dye No. 1). Soak 3 or 4 hours.

After treatment: Remove, press out extra dye. Shake out yarn and
dry; rinse in water to which has been added ½ cup of sumac
berry acid (water may be slightly alkaline). Remove, shake
out and dry.

Result: A fine, carmine-pink.

Test: Permanent to rinsing.

Recipe No. 9   For wool and cotton

KOKO'MA CARMINE-RED
koko'ma (Zea mays amylacea)

Use Stock Dye No. 1 or No. 3 (acid dye).

Mordanting: Bring to boil and boil gently for 15 minutes. Now
add enough water to bring the quantity up to 6 cups (1½ litres).

Material added: To this dye add 1 double handful (30-40 grams)
of wool or cotton soaked in sumac berry acid. Wool washed in
a neutral soap and rinsed. Cotton soaked in plain warm water
(non-alkaline).

Treatment in dye: Immerse in dye and bring to boiling point
slowly. Boil about 15 minutes. If dye turns dull, add more
sumac berry acid.

After treatment: Set aside and soak overnight. Remove from dye,
wring lightly and dry. Rinse in cold water after drying.

Result: Wool a fine, carmine-red.

Recipe No. 10   For cotton

KOKO'MA RASPBERRY-RED
koko'ma (Zea mays amylacea)

Preparation of material: Take cotton yarn or loose cotton, about 1 double handful (10 grams) and soak 24 hours in sumac berry acid, dry and then rinse. Prepare a solution of cream of tartar; 500 grams cream of tartar in water. Now immerse cotton in solution of cream of tartar and allow to soak ½ hour. Remove and press out extra liquid.

Material added: Immerse in carmine dye bath and soak 3 or 4 hours.

After treatment: Remove, press out dye and dry.

Result: Fine, deep, raspberry-red.

Remarks: If washed in alkaline water, will turn bluish.

Recipe No. 11   For wool and cotton
KOKO'MA RASPBERRY-RED
koko'ma (Zea mays amylacea)

Use Stock Dye No. 3.

Mordanting: Replace on fire and boil down slowly to ½ quantity of liquid. Now add ¾ cup (200 ml.) of sumac berry liquid. Add 1 handful (25 ml.) of ground native alum. Alum added to carmine dye after addition of sumac acid does not turn carmine dye purple. Boil ½ hour and add second ¾ cup (200 ml.) of berry liquid. Acid and alkali maintain a balance and dye remains stable. Color unchanged by boiling for any length of time. Not affected by cooling and reheating.

Material added: To 6 cups (1½ litres) of this dye add 1 double handful (30-40 grams) of wool or cotton washed in yucca suds then boiled ½ hour in alum water and rinsed.

Treatment in dye: Bring to boiling point slowly and boil 2 hours; or soak in dye overnight and boil for 1 hour.

After treatment: Remove from dye, wring lightly and dry. Rinse thoroughly.

Result: Wool, deep carmine or raspberry-red; cotton, fine pink.

Washing test: Wool, fairly fast, slightly more brownish; cotton, turns bluish.

Test No. 1.

Cotton and wool unwashed and soaked in liquid sheep manure, boiled in above dye, fine, deep, raspberry-red.

Test No. 2.

Cotton and wool smoked after dyeing, intensifies color.

Recipe No. 12   For wool and cotton
KOKO'MA MAROON
koko'ma (Zea mays amylacea)

Use Stock Dye No. 1.

Mordanting: Add to this, ½ cup (150 ml.) of liquid from sumac
berries, produced by boiling berries ½ hour or soaking 24
hours; 1 handful (20-25 grams) of berries in 1-1/3 cups (300
ml.) of water. Strain berries through cloth and squeeze out
juice. Replace on fire. Boil down to about 8 cups (2 litres).

Material added: To 8 cups (2 litres) of this dye add 1 double
handful (30-40 grams) of wool or cotton washed or soaked
in yucca suds.

Treatment in dye: Bring to boiling point slowly and boil gently
from 1-2 hours. Liquid will slowly lose brilliancy. Add ½ cup
(150 ml.) sumac berry liquid. Dye reaches stable phase.

After treatment: Remove from dye, wring slightly and dry. Rinse
thoroughly.

Result: Wool, a good, deep maroon; cotton, a good pink.

Washing test: Wool, fairly fast, slightly more bluish; cotton not
fast, turns blue.

Test No. 1

Use Stock Dye No. 1 and Recipe No. 12.
Substitute unwashed wool and cotton which has been soaked
in liquid sheep manure. (See Chapter V.)

Result: Wool, a good, deep maroon; cotton, a good pink.

Washing test: Wool, permanent; cotton, turns bluish.

Test No. 2

Use Stock Dye No. 1 and Recipe No. 12.
Substitute cotton washed and boiled a few minutes in plain
water. Immerse in dye. Soak 48 hours.

Result: Cotton, before rinsing, a very fine, brilliant maroon; turns
more bluish when rinsed.

Washing test: Not fast, will not stand soap.

Test No. 3

Use Stock Dye No. 1 and Recipe No. 12.

After treatment: When wool or cotton is removed from dye and wrung out, place at once in smoker. (See Chapter V.) Smoke about 10 minutes. Wool slightly darkened. Rinse thoroughly.

Result: Wool, good, dark maroon.

Washing test: Wool, fast; cotton, turns bluish.

Recipe No. 13   For wool and cotton

KOKO'MA BROWN
koko'ma (Zea mays amylacea)

Use Stock Dye No. 2.

Mordanting: Add to Stock Dye No. 2, ½ cup (150 ml.) of liquid from sumac berries, produced by boiling berries ½ hour or soaked 24 hours. 1 handful (20-25 grams) of berries in 1-1/3 cups (300 ml.) of water. Strain berries through cloth and squeeze out juice. Replace on fire. Boil down to about 6 cups (1½ litres).

Material added: To 6 cups (1½ litres) of this dye add 1 double handful (30-40 grams) of wool or cotton washed in yucca suds, then rinsed.

Treatment in dye: Bring to boiling point slowly and boil for 1-2 hours.

After treatment: Remove from dye, wring lightly and dry, then rinse thoroughly.

Result: Wool, a good, red-brown; cotton, fair.

Washing test: Wool, fairly fast, loses a little color; cotton, fair.

Recipe No. 14   For wool and cotton
KOKO'MA TAN
koko'ma (Zea mays amylacea)

Use Stock Dye No. 1.

Mordanting: Add ¾ cup (200 ml.) of sumac berry liquid; then add
1 handful (25 ml.) of ground native alum.

Material added: To 6 cups (1½ litres) of this dye add 1 double
handful (30-40 grams) of wool or cotton washed in yucca suds
and rinsed, then boiled with alum.

Treatment in dye: Immerse in dye, and bring to boiling point slowly. Boil 2 hours.

After treatment: Remove from dye, wring lightly and dry. Rinse
thoroughly.

Result: Wool, a dull pink-brown or tan; cotton, good pink-tan.
Note: If a second dip is required, the pan may be set upon
the stove and reheated but it must not be allowed to boil.

Test No. 1

Use Stock Dye No. 1 and Recipe No. 14.

Preparation of material: Substitute wool washed in yucca and
rinsed.

Treatment in dye: Immerse in dye, boil for 2 hours.

Result: Wool, light pink-tan.

Recipe No. 15   For wool and cotton
KOKO'MA BLUE
koko'ma (Zea mays amylacea)

Use Stock Dye No. 1.

Mordanting: Add ¾ cup (200 ml.) of sumac berry liquid. Liquid is intensified in color.

Material added: To 6 cups (1½ litres) of this dye add 1 double handful (30-40 grams) of wool washed in Lux soap and rinsed or cotton boiled in plain water.

Treatment in dye: Bring to boiling point slowly and remove from fire.

After treatment: Set aside and soak for 48 hours. Remove from dye, wring slightly and dry. Rinse thoroughly.

Result: Wool, a good blue; cotton, same.

Washing test: Wool, loses color; cotton, same.

CHAPTER XI

Greens

Vegetable dyes in which *two* colors are used to produce *one* shade

THE WRITER'S EXPERIMENTS and research have proved that two separate colors cannot be mixed together in the same dye pot, to produce a third color, such as yellow plus blue equals green, or blue plus red equals purple.

Provided a plant cannot be used which will produce the desired color in one operation such colors must then be produced in the following manner.

The two colors necessary to produce the third color are prepared in separate dye pots and the material, wool, cotton or basketry fibers, are dyed first in one color and then in the other. Thus the colors are *superimposed* one upon another, avoiding chemical reactions.

The resulting shades are clear and strong.

The material dyed, whatever it may be, must be allowed to dry before its immersion in the second dye.

After the material is dry and when it is ready to dip in the second color, it should first be soaked in warm water and lightly wrung out, then the material will take the dye more evenly. When used in a "two dye" process, indigo dye may be slightly warmed.

The recipes for "greens" in this paper are produced as described above.

Recipe No. 1   For wool and cotton

YELLOW ON BLUE
(Siva'pi Green and Indigo)

Use Indigo Blue Recipe No. 1.

Use Siva'pi Yellow Stock Dye No. 1.

Mordanting: Add to 8 cups of *siva'pi* yellow dye 1 small double handful (100 ml.) of ground alum. This mixture foams and the liquid turns opaque yellow.

Material added: To 8 cups (2 litres) of this dye add ½ hank of indigo dyed wool or cotton yarn soaked in warm water before immersing in dye.

Treatment in dye: Immerse in dye, bring to boil slowly and boil about 1 hour.

After treatment: Color is improved by soaking wool or cotton in dye overnight after boiling. Remove from dye, wring lightly and dry. Rinse thoroughly.

Result: A good, even, deep green.

Remarks: No yellow float which may be prevented by the overnight soaking.

Recipe No. 2   For wool
YELLOW ON BLUE (alternate)
(Siva'pi Green and Indigo)

Use Indigo Blue Recipe No. 1.

Use Siva'pi Yellow Stock Dye No. 1.

Mordanting: Add to Siva'pi Yellow Stock Dye No. 1 (alternate) 1 small double handful (100 ml.) of ground native alum — mixture foams.

Material added: To 4 cups (1 litre) of this dye add about 1 small handful or ½ hank (20 grams) of spun yarn dyed in Indigo Blue Recipe No. 1. This should be first soaked in warm water for a few moments to remove air bubbles before immersing in the *siva'pi* dye.

Treatment in dye: Immerse in dye, bring to boiling point slowly and boil 1 hour.

After treatment: Remove from dye, wring thoroughly and dry. Rinse well in warm water after drying.

Result: Wool, a good, dark green, but yellow overlay on blue quite evident.

Recipe No. 3   For wool and cotton
BLUE ON YELLOW
(Siva'pi and Indigo Green)

Use Siva'pi Yellow Stock Dye No. 1.

Use Recipes Nos. 1 or 2 and Indigo Blue Recipe No. 1.

Mordanting: Take 1 large double handful (50 grams) of dyed *siva'pi* yellow wool.

Material added: Soak in lukewarm water, wring lightly and immerse in indigo blue dye pot.

Treatment in dye: Stir thoroughly and treat as in Indigo Blue Recipe No. 1. Soak from 12 to 48 hours, depending upon the shade of green desired. Shades from a gold-green to a deep, blue-green can be produced, depending upon the period of immersion.

After treatment: Remove, wring lightly and dry in the open air. Rinse thoroughly after drying.

Result: Wool, a good green; cotton, fair. The blue of the indigo superimposed upon the yellow of the *siva'pi* produces fine shades of green. (This is the preferred method.) The reverse process shows film of imposed yellow on the indigo, (except when soaked overnight). Indigo dye should never be boiled.

For basketry (wicker)
GREEN
(Siva'pi Green and Indigo)

Wicker basketry material may be successfully dyed green by immersing first in *siva'pi* yellow dye, and later in a bath of indigo blue. (If the process is reversed, there will be a "float" of yellow on the dyed indigo. For one exception, see Recipe No. 1, Yellow on Blue.)

1. Yellow dye bath

For this purpose allow the material to dry before dyeing in indigo. If desired, it can be smoked while still damp (see smoking), and then dyed in indigo. (See recipe "Siva'pi Indigo.")

2. Indigo dye bath

The indigo dye is *not heated.* The basketry material is immersed in the cool dye and handled just as it is described above for *siva'pi* yellow. When finished, this color is *not smoked.*

3. *Saqwa* — Indigo dip — light green*

Dip basketry material in indigo and soak and then smoke this with white wool and flowers of *siva'pi.*
Result: Light green.

If you use same recipe with dark wool — dark green.

* This recipe was not tested by the writer.

For basketry
SIVA'PI AND TUPENMORI — GREEN
(*Chrysothamnus* sp. and *Phaseolus vulgaris*)

Basketry material dyed as in Siva'pi Yellow Recipe No. 1. Place this dyed material in the blue dye of the blue-black bean, and remove when turning green.

Place at once in a smoker. If this material does not become green enough when smoked, dip in dye again and smoke once more.
Result: A nice, apple-green.

The *siva'pi* yellow basket material must *not* be allowed to boil in hot bean dye; simply heated and then removed from stove. If allowed to boil, the yellow will boil out before the blue has time to penetrate.

CHAPTER XII

Blacks

THERE ARE TWO PRINCIPAL ways of making black dye and, of course, there are individual minor variations in these methods. Both recipes are given, although the chemical principle is the same in each.

In both cases, the chief factors are iron and tannin, which together produce a blue-black ink or dye.

In both recipes the insoluble yellow ochre or (limonite) iron hydroxide is reduced to a soluble form by burning the ore with gum of the pinyon tree. This process produces a fine black soot or powder which is soluble in water.

The tannin is produced in two forms:

(1) From the seeds of the black seeded Indian sunflower *(Helianthus* sp.).

(2) From the leaves and branchlets of *su:'vi,* or sumac *(Rhus trilobata).*

How the intricate chemical principle involved in this process was discovered by the Hopi, and probably by other tribes of the Southwest,* will always remain an intriguing mystery.

Cotton, wool and basketry materials are all dyed with these dyes.

When "Sunflower Seed — Iron Black" is used, natural black or brown wool is always used instead of white, as the shade of black produced on this is more intense.

Cotton does not take this dye well. Basketry material, however, can be dyed a good blue-black.

The black-seeded sunflower is a cultivated plant, it is grown in

_____
* Also used by Navajo (Bryan and Young, 1940, pp. 65-67).

northern Arizona at an altitude of about 4,500 feet, in semi-desert country.

"Sumac — Iron Black" is usually dyed on dark wool and this dye will also dye cotton a good black. It is successful on basketry material.

For basketry

(a) BLACK
'A:'qaw'u or Sunflower Seed (*Helianthus* sp.) and
Yellow Ochre (iron hydroxide)

(b) BLACK OR BLUE
su:'vi or Sumac (*Rhus trilobata*) and Iron

Both methods of producing black dye can be used successfully on basketry material, both wicker and yucca types.

Dyeing

The mordanted dye is allowed to cool until nearly lukewarm, in a receptacle long and deep enough to accommodate the length of the material (10-15 inches). The stems or strips are immersed in this dye bath either loose or tied lightly in bundles. The vessel is gently agitated at intervals and the bundles turned so that the dye will take evenly on the material.

Black basketry material is not smoked after dyeing.

Stock Dye No. 1

(a) BLACK

(iron, from pinyon gum and yellow ochre (iron hydroxide)
and sunflower seed *(Helianthus* sp.)

Part 1

Take lumps of pinyon gum as free of dirt as possible. Melt in
an iron pan or kettle and strain through a cloth or fine sieve.
Prepare this outdoors. (The Hopi strained pinyon gum through
coarse horse tail hair, etc.) Replace melted gum in a long-
handled iron frying pan and bring to boil. This should be done
over a fire outdoors also, as this smoke injures the throat.
Melted gum — about 2 cups (400 ml.). Grind about 1 large
double handful (150 ml.) of lump ochre (limonite) to powder
on a stone mortar, a little at a time. Add this powder to the
boiling pinyon gum and stir constantly until the mass darkens
and thickens. Allow the mixture to boil down or to "catch fire,"
and continue to stir with a long stick. In 15 or 20 minutes the
mass will blacken and turn crisp. Remove from fire, and grind
charred mass to fine, black powder on a stone mortar.

Result: Thus the iron in the limonite or ochre has now been reduced to a form soluble in water.

Part 2

Take purple sunflower seed — 1 large double handful (150 ml.).
Water — 8 cups (2 litres). Bring to boil slowly. Boil gently ½
hour or until seeds begin to crack open. Remove from fire
and strain.

Result: Deep, reddish-purple liquid.

Part 3

Add to this about 1 small double handful (100 ml.) of ground
native alum. Dye liquid at once turns a deep, blue-purple.
Now add to this liquid 1 small double handful (100 ml.) of
the oxide-pinyon gum powder. Stir well and boil ½ hour.

Result: This dye should be a fine, rich blue-black ink. The principle
of the gum-ochre powder is iron, which forms an ink when
combined with the tannin in the sunflower dye.

Stock Dye No. 2
(b) BLACK
su:'vi (Rhus trilobata) and limonite
(Pinyon gum, yellow ochre and sumac)
Part 1

Fill a 4-quart kettle with the crushed branchlets and leaves of sumac. Boil slowly about 4 hours, when the tannin in this liquid will be very strong.

Part 2

Prepare pinyon gum and yellow ochre as in Black (a). To 6 cups (1½ litres) of this liquid from the sumac branches, add about 80 grams of pinyon gum powder. The liquid at once turns to a black ink. Boil for a few minutes, and add brown or black wool, or cotton. Boil 3-4 hours. Remove, wring out, dry and rinse thoroughly.

Result: Wool, a good black; cotton, similar.*

* The Navajo use the same method to obtain a good black (Bryan and Young, 1940, pp. 65-67).

Recipe No. 1   For wool and cotton
BLACK
Sunflower Seed *(Helianthus* sp.*)* and Yellow Ochre
Use Stock Dye No. 1.

Material added: To 6 cups (1½ litres) of this dye, add 1 double handful (40 grams) of dark brown or black wool (never white) washed in yucca suds.

Treatment in dye: Bring to boil slowly, and boil gently 4 hours, stirring frequently.

After treatment: Remove, wring out slightly and dry. Rinse thoroughly, after drying.

Result: Wool, a fine blue-black; cotton, when treated with this dye, produces a dirty gray.

Recipe No. 2   For wool
BLACK
Sunflower Seed *(Helianthus* sp.*)* and Yellow Ochre

Use Stock Dye No. 1.

Mordanting: Add to this liquid 1 small double handful (100 ml.) of ground native alum. Dye at once turns a deep blue-purple.

Material added: To 6 cups (1½ litres) of this dye, add 1 double handful (40 grams) of wool or cotton. Use unwashed wool from which the dirt has been shaken out. Fill a quart jar with juniper ashes; then pour into the jar as much water as it will hold. Let this settle overnight. Pour off in morning, and in this liquid soak wool which has been dyed. This will set the color.

Recipe No. 3   For wool
BLACK (jet) and BLUE (pale)
'A:*'qaw'u* — Sunflower Seed *(Helianthus* sp.*)*

Pinyon gum, 3 to 5 pounds. Boil down pinyon gum in a pot, add sulphur powder which is found in association with native coal. Stir constantly until the mass becomes dusty dry. Sunflower seed *('a:'qaw'u)* is boiled down and strained. The pinyon gum and sulphur mixture is added and the mixture is again boiled.

Result: This produces a jet black dye, which, if used diluted, will make a gray-blue dye.

REFERENCES

AMSDEN, C. A.

1934 *Navaho Weaving, its Technic and History.* The Fine Arts Press in cooperation with the Southwest Museum. Santa Ana, California.

BRYAN, N. G. and STELLA YOUNG

1940 *Navajo Native Dyes, Their Preparation and Use.* U. S. Office of Indian Affairs, Indian Handicrafts, No. 2. Chilocco Agricultural School, Chilocco, Oklahoma.

COLTON, M. R. F.

1932 Wool for Our Indian Weavers — What Shall It Be? *Museum Notes,* Vol. 4, No. 12. Museum of Northern Arizona, Flagstaff, Arizona.

KENT, KATE PECK

1957 *The Cultivation and Weaving of Cotton in the Pre-historic Southwestern United States.* Trans. of the A.P.S. n.s. Vol. 47, Part 3, pp. 457-732. American Philosophical Society, Philadelphia.

MAERZ, A., and M. REA PAUL

1930 *A Dictionary of Color.* McGraw-Hill, New York.

WHITING, A. F.

1939 Ethnobotany of the Hopi. *Bulletin* 15. Northern Arizona Society of Science and Art, Inc., Flagstaff, Arizona.

SUGGESTED READINGS

ADROSKO, RITA J.

1971 *Natural Dyes and Home Dyeing.* Dover Publications, New York.

BEMIS, ELIJAH

1815 *The Dyer's Companion.* Evert Duycknick, New York. Reprinted in 1973 by Dover Publications with an introduction by Rita Adrosko.

BLISS, ANNE

1976 *Rocky Mountain Dye Plants.* Johnson Printing Co., Boulder, Colorado.

BROOKLYN BOTANIC GARDEN

1973 Natural Plant Dying. Brooklyn Botanic Garden Record, *Plants and Gardens,* Vol. 29, No. 2. Also printed as a separate.

CONNER, BERENICE GILLETTE
  1975 *Dyes From Your Garden.* E.A. Seeman Publishing Co.,
      Miami, Florida.
FURRY, MARGARET S. and BESS M. VIEMONT
  1935 *Home Dyeing with Natural Dyes.* United States Depart-
      ment of Agriculture, Washington, D.C.
KRAMER, JACK
  1972 *Natural Dyes: Plants and Processes.* Charles Scribner's
      Sons, New York.
KROCHMAL, ARNOLD and CONNIE
  1974 *The Complete Illustrated Book of Dyes from Natural
      Sources.* Doubleday and Co., Inc., New York.
LAS ARANAS SPINNERS and WEAVERS GUILD
  1973 *Dyeing with Natural Materials.* Las Aranas, Albuquerque.
LESCH, ALMA
  1970 *Vegetable Dyeing: 151 Color Recipes for Dyeing Yarns and
      Fabrics with Natural Material.* Watson-Guptill Publica-
      tions, New York.
SCHULTZ, KATHLEEN
  1975 *Create Your Own Natural Dyes.* Sterling Publishing Co.,
      New York.

Other related publications include:

Shuttle, Spindle and Dyepot. Handweavers Guild of America
    publication, 998 Farmington Ave., West Hartford, CT 06107
    (quarterly).
Suppliers Directory. Handweavers Guild of America publication,
    988 Farmington Ave., West Hartford, CT 06107 (annual listing).
Interweave. Linda C. Lignon publication, 2938 N. County Rd. 13,
    Loveland, CO 80537 (quarterly).